_un_FINISHED BUSINESS

Eddie,
Keep pursuing your dreams!
I believe in you!

Heb 12:1-3

Eddie!
Never give up on your dreams...
Ever! Terry
1 cor 9:24

unFINISHED BUSINESS

A Book by

LEVI & TERRY GURNO

TERRYGURNO.COM

For permission requests, please address
Cedar Forge Press
7300 W. Joy Road
Dexter, MI 48130

Published 2018 by Cedar Forge
Printed in the United States of America

20 19 18   1 2 3 4
ISBN 978-1-943290-73-4
Library of Congress Control Number: 2018946721

TABLE OF CONTENTS

PART FOUR HOW BAD DO YOU WANT IT?

PART FIVE: FINISHED BUSINESS

— DEDICATION —

We dedicate this book to our family:
Nancy Gurno, Sarah Gurno
Chelsea Gurno, Ali and Christian Klundt

Anyone who has competed in an event like Ironman knows it takes a commitment from the entire family to finish. Their sacrifice for the dream is just as big and their support is crucial to putting in the hours it takes to train. The encouragement and support of our family never wavered. They yelled, cheered, prayed and believed . . .

. . . all the way to the finish.

"It is not the critic who counts; not the man who points out how the strong man stumbles, or where the doer of deeds could have done better. The credit belongs to the man who is actually in the arena, whose face is marred by dust and sweat and blood; who strives valiantly; who errs; who comes up short again and again...but who does actually strive to do the deeds...who at the best knows in the end the triumph of high achievement, and who at the worst, if he fails, at least fails while daring greatly, so that his place shall never be with those cold and timid souls who neither know victory nor defeat."

—THEODORE ROOSEVELT

Iron Sharpens Iron

IRONMAN IS CONSIDERED the world's toughest triathlon, pitting the mind and body against the human spirit. An
IRONMAN event consists of a 2.4-mile swim, 112-mile bike ride
and 26.2-mile run—all completed in 17 hours or less.

When in Coeur d'Alene, Idaho for the 2016 IRONMAN, I
came across a story about Terry and Levi Gurno on the front page
of the local newspaper. The story recounted Terry's first failed
attempt at IRONMAN in 2015, and how he was back this year
for another shot.

The article mentioned Terry was a motivational speaker. I
thought, "We have a story here, and I bet this guy Terry can tell it
well!" Terry was contacted, to see if he'd share his tale of redemp-
tion at our IRONMAN Welcome Ceremony. We figured it was a
longshot, since the ceremony was the next night—but there was
something about the article that told me Terry wouldn't back down
or give up that easy.

Once Terry started telling his story that night, I knew my intuition was right: he was the perfect person to inspire other athletes.

To rewind the story a bit: Terry and Levi tackled IRONMAN together in 2015, but they didn't have the race they intended the first time around. Terry's return to IRONMAN the second time is the epitome of unfinished business.

People assume you must be an elite athlete to compete in a race of this caliber, but IRONMAN athletes are normal, everyday people accomplishing an unimaginable goal. First-time IRONMAN athletes are typically super-nervous, pre-race, so hearing Terry's words of persistence and grit and never allowing oneself to surrender were helpful in calming their nerves and inspiring our athletes to never give up.

IRONMAN's mantra is *Anything Is Possible*—we've witnessed some amazing human beings pushing themselves to create their own possible through the last 13 years, but Terry made the 2016 IRONMAN Coeur d'Alene truly unforgettable.

In the last hour of an IRONMAN dreams really do come true. The athletes remaining on the course have been out there longer than anyone, and have pushed their bodies to the brink of endurance.

Looking down the finisher's chute and back at the clock, knowing that Terry was our last athlete on the course and worrying he wouldn't make the cut-off, then seeing him come staggering down the road—listing to the right but moving forward toward the finish line—that's the personification of IRONMAN. I remember thinking at the time this couldn't have been scripted better—Terry inspires our athletes prior to the race about never giving up, and here he is potentially our final finisher of the day.

*un*FINISHED BUSINESS—Terry and Levi's journey culminates in those last few minutes of the race. It was exciting, nerve-racking and inspiring all at once, a classic father-and-son story about two unlikely heroes overcoming the odds.

It begins at the end, when it looked like Terry and Levi's impossible dream would be over before it even began.

—DAVE DOWNEY,
IRONMAN TRACK ANNOUNCER

The Last Man Standing

IT'S NEARLY MIDNIGHT. All Terry Gurno can see, in any direction, is darkness.

A hot August wind races through downtown Coeur d'Alene. The wind pounds off the storefronts on Sherman Avenue, rushing in like ocean waves crashing down on Terry, surging over the hills and streets he has climbed. Spreading out behind him is mile after lonesome mile of the Ironman race course.

For two years, Terry has trained to conquer this immense challenge—the grueling, 140.6-mile Ironman triathlon! He has swum 2.4 miles, and biked 112 miles. Now he is on foot, running and hobbling and gasping. It feels like he has been gasping for the past 17 hours. He is five blocks from the finish line. When the day started, there were more than a thousand Ironman competitors on the course. Now, Terry is the last one.

And he has nothing left.

Every other athlete in the race has either finished or been disqualified, and been cleared from the course. Competitors have pumped their fists at the finish line on Sherman Avenue, fallen into the arms of their spouses and children, and gone home.

All except Ironman Competitor #1662, Terry Gurno.

Terry is the last man standing.

The last competitor Terry passed was minutes ago, as Terry stumbled out of deserted McEuen Park and crossed the bridge to Fourth Street. The look in the guy's eyes as Terry lumbered past said it all: *Buddy, you're not gonna make it.*

I must look bad, Terry thinks to himself, as he tries to clear his head and gasps for air. Trying to get his legs moving again to finish the race.

Up ahead at the finish line somewhere, Terry hears screams. He hears the shrieks of the crowd, chanting, clapping, pounding the barriers and the sidewalk. He looks up and sees the race clock is turned off. Terry's eyes loll about in dazed bewilderment. He wonders if he's been disqualified, if the race officials have given him up for dead, unwilling to witness him pushing through the pain just to stumble home in defeat again.

As Terry lumbers up the street he looks down at his body. His neon-yellow cycling shirt is stained with salt from his own sweat. His legs, burned by the sun, look skinny and useless. His kidneys ache with each step. His lungs are ready to burst. Terry's 55-year-old body that trained so hard has shrunken, and let him down.

Five blocks from the finish line, Terry's ready to give up. His dream—the dream of every man, to fight a great battle and emerge in victory—is in danger of being dashed.

I am failing again, Terry thinks to himself. *Just like last year.* His battle is lost. He is letting down his family, his friends, his supporters, even the strangers on the Ironman course who have been rooting for this crazy man—snapping photographs, clapping, waving, cheering Terry on as he ran. In his head he hears the voice of his old baseball coach, whispering to him, telling him he's a loser, like the guy did when Terry quit the team in the 9th grade.

Shutting out the voices, Terry prays to himself, for strength. *God help me!*

There is a terrific roaring sound. Terry realizes it is the track announcer, up on Sherman. The end of his race is close! In his mind he hears his son Levi screaming, "Dad, come *on!!*" Then all the voices seem to shrink away, just as Terry's body seems to be shrinking away underneath him.

What are you doing, Gurno? Terry's thoughts scream. *Suck it up. You have unfinished business.*

Spurred, Terry looks up toward the finish line, and starts running again. Running faster. He knows he doesn't have time to waste. So he pushes himself, though he can barely stay upright on the course now, his legs floundering, weaving and staggering in excruciating pain.

The pain eats at Terry. His knees feel like they've been torn apart. His eyes blur in tears. Gasping for air he coughs, sputters, gasps again, his brain pulsing with panic. He feels like a machine that is falling apart piece by piece and breaking down.

As Terry staggers toward the dazzling lights of the finish line, the emotions hit in a wave that nearly drowns him. Terror, fear, anxiety bombard his mind. Terry's heart sags.

This is death, his overloaded brain tells him, lumbering to run faster. *This is the death of my dream.*

Somewhere beneath him his exhausted feet slap the black pavement. The wind has stopped. It suddenly seems cold. Terry veers left and right then stumbles forward, racing the clock that's no longer ticking, alone. He weaves and sags and is about to keel over. Out of his gasping heart rises a question:

Why did I do this?

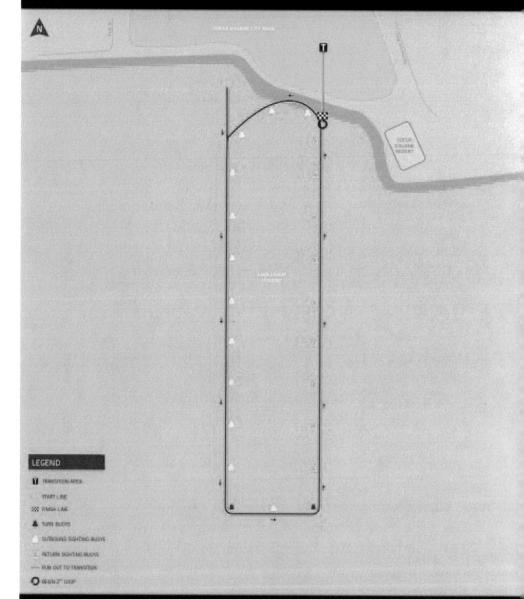

PART ONE

THE BIRTH OF THE DREAM

Chapter One

Terry's Story

TERRY: I figure if a guy like me can overcome all the curveballs life has thrown and beat all the odds, then anybody can.

My father was an alcoholic. So was his entire family—his siblings, and his parents. Because of that, my childhood was violent, and abusive in every way. Our home was not a safe place. The only time we felt safe was if my dad wasn't home.

We lived on Morningside Street, in Long Beach, California. A little pink house, just over the bridge from Compton. I had four siblings—two older brothers, and two younger sisters. I was the middle child.

My brothers and I all shared a bedroom that was a converted garage. My sisters stayed in another room that was . . . well, it really wasn't a bedroom. It didn't have a door. From our bedroom, you would enter through this little breezeway into our sisters' bedroom, which was just this big square room.

We were not a close family in terms of touching or hugging. Nobody in my family ever said, "I love you."

I never had moments with my dad. I didn't know what it was like to have a dad like the fathers I saw on TV—a dad who cared, listened, laughed, spent time with me.

I didn't have that.

And I really, *really* wanted it.

My dad would drop me off somewhere, then never come back to pick me up. He'd take me to football practice and never return. It would be dark and I'd end up walking home, a ten-year-old boy, scared out of my mind. I remember other times being with him on a Saturday, and he'd stop at a tavern and drink for hours and hours and we kids would just have to wait. Finally, dad would come out and get in the car and drive us home. I remember how scared we all were, watching him weave all over the road from the back seat.

He beat all of us kids. He beat my mother. There were a few times growing up when we didn't know if our mother would live through some of the beatings she took.

Dad's anger was vicious. The beatings were brutal. They never seemed to stop. One day, I came home late from school. My dad met me at the door. There was a dog chain on the porch and he was upset. He picked up that dog chain and started beating me with it. I remember running around the house to get away while my dad whipped me and beat me.

Violence seemed to erupt out of my dad. If it wasn't one thing, it was another. We were completely at his mercy.

You'd look at my dad wrong. *Boom!* He'd knock you down. If you looked away—*Boom!* He'd give you another crack. I'd watch my siblings staggering to their feet thinking, *Why would a guy do that, to his own kids?*

When I was ten, our family moved to Renton, Washington. The beatings kept coming. Finally, my mom realized she'd had enough.

She gathered all of us together one night and packed her bags and said she was leaving, because she felt if she stayed she may not survive.

"Now I'm going downstairs," Mom said, "'til I hear your dad come home, because I don't want to leave you kids alone. When I hear him come in the door, I'll leave."

I went to bed thinking, *I'm not going to see my mom anymore.* I lay in bed praying Mom didn't fall asleep, before Dad came home. She did. He found her with her suitcase. I'll never forget the sounds of the violence, that night.

Shortly thereafter, my dad finally left us. He didn't officially say, "I'm out of here"—he just didn't come home one night. We were okay with that. I found out later my dad was having an affair. He was staying just a few blocks away. He kept it a secret, then left our mom to deal with the reality.

In all this chaos, I don't ever remember my mom badmouthing my dad. She never talked negative about him. She just went to work and tried to do the best she could, raising five kids on her own, with no help from my dad. She started working double shifts, seven days a week, as a waitress. She'd work a lunch shift and then work the evening shift. After she was done waitressing, she'd bartend until two in the morning. So we really didn't see our mom much, even when we were young.

I began to struggle with not being a "normal" kid. I began seeing myself as a dumb kid. A stupid kid.

My teachers didn't know I had a learning disability. I tried hard to learn to read, but it was like my brain went to sleep. I started getting taunted by the other kids. They called me "stupid" and "dummy" and "not smart," so I was taken out of the regular classroom, and put in a class for slow learners.

As I got into junior high, things got worse.

Whenever there was a contest or you teamed up in school,

nobody wanted me because I wasn't smart. They placed me in special reading groups and I still couldn't read. When I was in ninth
grade, I was going to be the starting catcher on our varsity baseball
team. One day, my coach pulled me aside. "Gurno," he said, "your
progress report is out. You're not doing well. In fact, if you don't
bring your grades up, you're not going to be able to play."

The next day I went back to my coach and turned in my uniform
and said, "Coach, I quit." I didn't *want* to quit, because sports was
all I had. My dad was gone. My mom was working overtime, so she
wasn't home. None of us kids ever wanted to be home. Everybody
found other places to be, other things to do. Sports was *my* thing.
It was my security and my comfort.

The problem was, I knew I couldn't get my grades up. I wasn't
smart—I was stupid, I was dumb. The only choice I felt I had was
to quit.

The coach held no sympathy for me. He said, "Gurno, you're a
loser. You'll always be a loser. Get out of my office."

Even with all of that stuff going around, I tried to stay positive.
I wouldn't let it get me down.

No matter what I did though, the word *loser* stuck with me. It
deflated me. It started to kill all my dreams. The Bible says words
have the power of life and death in them.

There were not a lot of words of life coming my way.

By the time I graduated from high school, I was functionally
illiterate. I knew college wasn't an option. I had no direction for my
life. I felt like my life needed a do-over.

One day, a friend called and said, "Hey, you want to go to church?"

"Sure," I said. The only reason I said yes is because I didn't have
anything else to do. My future looked hopeless. I had no direction.
I was bored. I went to church and I heard this very simple message
of the Gospel. I heard God's Word, crying out to me. It gave me
hope. It spoke to me, I understood it, and I responded to it. In the

middle of everything I felt God calling to me, "Terry, you can have a second chance." I felt God's forgiveness. I felt the constant battle with my past suddenly healing.

When the pastor asked us to close our eyes and pray, I closed my eyes and prayed my heart out to God.

As I was praying I heard the pastor say, "If you're here today and you want to receive Christ, just raise your hand and I'll pray for you."

My hand shot up.

"Okay, I see that hand, I see that hand." Because there were a bunch of hands going up and I didn't know if the pastor saw *my* hand, I started waving it, back and forth.

"Yes, I see that," he said. "Yes, I see it." Meanwhile my hand is still waving back and forth. Basically what I was saying is, *Don't miss me. Please God, don't miss me!* I didn't want him to miss my hand.

Afterwards I went up to receive Christ. I knew my life had changed. I didn't know how yet, but I felt like a new person.

I started going to a small group, a Bible study. There, a guy named Bob, an engineer at Boeing, would open up the Bible and we'd talk about life.

Bob picked up on some of my language. He overheard me saying things like, "People like me don't get to do stuff like that," or "I could never be able to do that."

Bob pulled me aside and asked me why I talked that way. "Where is that coming from?"

I shrugged. Bob's question gave me an odd feeling. But Bob kept at me.

"Terry," he said, "you're not dumb. You're not stupid. Stop believing that stuff. You're *smart.*" And he told me why he believed that.

For whatever reason, it made sense to me. Deep down, I didn't think I was stupid. I had just been told my whole life that I was.

Bob was the first person who ever talked to me that way. He said, "What is it you really want to do?"

"I really want to go to college. I want to get my degree." It was like the words crawled right out of my mouth.

"Then you should go, Terry," Bob insisted. "I believe in you. I believe you can do that."

The next day I applied to the closest private college. Because I'm part Native American, on my dad's side, and the BIA was going to pay for my college education, I was accepted. It definitely wasn't because of my grades.

Bob's words gave me the courage to go to school, but that didn't make it easy. I didn't know it then, but I had dyslexia. After my first quarter in college I was put on academic probation. Still, I believed what Bob had told me—I wasn't dumb. I knew I could learn and I didn't give up. Five years later, I became the first person in my family to graduate with their bachelor's degree.

It was in the beginning of my second year at college when I happened to notice a girl sitting in front of me in chapel.

Honestly, I must have stared at this girl for a long time. She had the most beautiful head of hair I'd ever seen. *Terry,* I thought, *you've got to meet this girl. You've got to meet the person who owns this hair.*

I tapped her on the shoulder and she turned around. I said, "Hey, my name's Terry."

"I'm Nancy," she said. I kept staring at her hair.

"Nice to meet you, Nancy," I blurted out, and we just started talking.

We'd see each other on campus and talk. Nancy was the most kind, caring, positive person I'd ever met. I knew that's the kind of person I needed in my life.

From that day on, I couldn't get Nancy out of my head. One day, I noticed she wasn't in class. She wasn't in chapel. I was worried, so I went over to her dorm and buzzed her room.

Nancy came out. She didn't have any makeup on. She was wearing this lime-green shirt, with a lavender raincoat. She had on a pair of old blue jeans. I looked at her and thought, *This is the girl I'm going to marry. This is her.*

A year later, I asked Nancy to marry me.

Around that same time I started reconnecting with my dad.

By now, he was living in Anacortes, Washington. He called and asked me to come up and see him at Christmas. "Okay," I said, because there's always a part of you that wants to connect with your dad.

On the drive up, I imagined what that night would be like. I pictured my dad sitting me down and saying, "Son, tell me about your life and where you've been." I was excited.

When I got there, my dad came to the door. "Follow me," he grunted, walked right past me, and got in his car. I followed him down the road to this house where there was a wild party going on. It was drugs. It was drinking. It was not my scene at all, and never had been. I was so angry. I stayed there awhile and then said, "Dad, I'm leaving."

He followed me outside. I turned around and said, "You know what, Dad? I'm ashamed of you. I've been more of a father to you than you've ever been to me. I don't ever want to see you again until you're sober." Then I walked off.

As I was driving down I-5 going back to college, this thought just broke my heart. I started thinking about my dad growing up as a child. I knew that my grandma was incredibly abusive to him. She was an alcoholic and she beat him. I realized my dad's just like me. He's a victim. My dad has been hurt, too.

The next year, my dad asked me to come up again for Christmas. He hadn't changed, but I had. I was no longer upset or angry. In fact, I felt compassion for him.

This year the party was at his house. I stayed awhile, then got up to leave. My dad followed me out of the house and asked me if I was still ashamed of him.

"No, Dad," I said, "I love you."

He looked at me and said, "I'm going to change, son, I promise."

I looked my dad in the eye and replied, "I know you will."

One day at college I got a call. This was when they had payphones in the hallway. "Hey, Terry, it's your dad!"

I picked up the phone. I took a deep breath before answering. "Hi, Dad," I finally said.

"Hey, son," I heard my dad say. Something about his voice sounded different. "I'm calling you for a couple of reasons. Number one, I was told I needed to tell somebody. Number two, you came to my mind right away. Number three, you need to hear this from me and nobody else. I just want you to know I was in church this morning, and I committed my life to Christ."

I was stunned. I felt this roar of adrenaline pumping through me.

A few months later, Dad asked me to baptize him. That's when I really began to see my dad's life change.

We started talking more. I started seeing him more. All those old bridges I'd thought we'd burned were being rebuilt. Sure, we still had old unfinished business. What I realized was the unfinished business wasn't going back in time. The unfinished business was starting from that point moving *forward*.

When I was in high school, the thing I wanted most in life was the one thing I never had growing up. And that was *a family. My* family. I never wanted my kids to know the pain I grew up with. I didn't want them to be afraid. I wanted to give them what I always wished I would have had.

Approval.

Protection.

Love.

I made a commitment to never be like my dad had been. When Nancy and I were pregnant with our first child, Chelsea, I went through a time of questioning. One day I asked Nancy, "Do you think I will know how to love my kids?" It was a big fear. Everyone says a child changes your life. I was worried I couldn't provide the kind of love a child would need.

People deal with life's curveballs differently. Being a father was the biggest curveball I'd ever been thrown. I was excited and scared at the same time. But Nancy rallied to the challenge. She trusted that everything in our lives would fall perfectly into place. As new parents, we couldn't have been happier or more excited. We were both determined to overcome whatever obstacle was put in our way.

After Chelsea, we had two more children. The third was our daughter, Alizabeth—Ali, for short.

In-between the two girls, our son Levi came into our lives...

CHAPTER TWO

Levi's Story

TERRY: We called Levi "Mr. Personality." You can see it in his baby photos—even when he was three months old, he'd put on a big smile for the camera.

That was just Levi. He had that beautiful *smile.*

Everywhere Levi went, he made friends. He was talkative. He was inquisitive. He wanted to know about people. He wanted to know their names. He made friends with anybody and everybody.

LEVI: My dad always said I was a born storyteller. I liked to entertain people. I was a kid who gathered people together, a connector. It's probably a middle-child thing, but I wanted everybody to be included.

TERRY: Levi wanted everybody to be a part of any fun that was going on. He felt bad if somebody was missing out on what was happening.

LEVI: I've always looked out for anyone who was on the outside, and tried to bring them on the inside. Tried to make them feel like they're a part of it.

TERRY: We moved to Coeur d'Alene when Levi was seven. They were building new homes in our development. Levi watched the construction going on and quickly figured everything out.

"You know, Dad," he said, "I was thinking. If I made coffee, if I get some juice, some donuts, and some muffins, I could probably walk around all these construction guys and I bet I could make some money selling stuff to them."

"Yeah," Nancy and I said, "you probably could."

So Levi did. He went around the construction site, meeting the guys and talking to them and starting his little entrepreneurial career at a young age.

We used to do a garage sale every year. That way, our kids could sell stuff and have their own spending money for vacation. All the kids set up their own tables. Levi would set up his table. He was the only one who would say to the customers, "Hey, come on, mister, come on over! We got some great stuff here on the table." The girls would be quiet, but Levi's "Hey come on over. You guys are gonna like what you see."

One time this lady was looking around and said, "What I'm really looking for are some horses." Well, Levi had a collection of toy horses. He looked at her and said, "Horses? I'll be right back!" He ran to his room and came out with a whole collection of horses. "Here you go, I've got horses." Just like that. He's a real connector with people.

Things began to change around the time Levi hit seven years old.

LEVI: At age six, I was diagnosed with asthma.

I was always an active kid, when I was younger. But as I got asthma, it really slowed me down. My energy level wasn't the same.

My activities weren't the same. What happens when some people start taking Albuterol—which is a steroid medication for asthma patients—is they experience weight-gain.

I was one of those people.

At age 13, I found myself at 240 pounds. I was insecure, so I lost a lot of confidence. But on the outside people never would have known that, because I came off as confident to mask my insecurities.

I was always the class clown. I didn't want people to know I was insecure, so even when I would get made fun of for being over-weight or slow or fat, I would laugh with people. But inside, it affected me a lot. And this carried on through high school.

In high school, I started getting a little more active. My fresh-man year came around, and I had lost a little weight, but I was still big. I was what you call football big, hefty. My insecurities kicked into an even higher gear, and that continued through high school.

TERRY: Levi lost confidence in himself, because of having asthma and gaining weight. He started blaming himself. Blaming the peo-ple around him.

He'd always been Mr. Personality. He'd always been outgoing, an encourager. But now he was going more inward. He was fighting a battle inside himself. He began to struggle with his mindset.

LEVI: I found myself constantly trying to find my security in other things, whether that be relationships, popularity, sports, being funny, friendships, just anything I could latch onto. I wanted to find security in something, because in and of myself, I was very insecure. I was not confident. I was super-unhappy with myself.

Midway through my junior year, I was still tipping the scales at 240 pounds. I was sick of being overweight. I wanted to get in shape for a lot of reasons—for sports, to not be made fun of anymore, to just feel better, to look better. Over the course of six months I ended up dropping 70 pounds through exercise. I had a personal trainer. I was up every morning before school at 5:00. I'd get up before dawn and I'd run three or four miles.

TERRY: Levi really started working out. Running. Exercising. He was extremely disciplined, and we had never seen that before. It was all about Levi not feeling good about himself and wanting to be healthy.

LEVI: I would lift weights at school and go to the gym. My life revolved around exercise, which I look back now and that was just another way of just masking my insecurities, my pain.

TERRY: The problem was, even though he looked fantastic, Levi struggled with his mindset. He had a new look, but the same old negative mindset.

LEVI: Here I'd lost all that weight—I was down to 165 pounds and people would say, "Man, you look *amazing*." And it felt good. I had a lot of energy, but my insecurities didn't go away.

In fact, they got *worse*.

I still looked at myself as fat. As overweight. That's who I saw when I looked in the mirror. I would come home from school and change out of my school clothes. I'd look in the mirror and honestly hate what I saw to a point where I would cry. I'd lay down on my bed and say, "Man, I hate myself!"

TERRY: It was not a good place for Levi to be. All that negative self-talk took up all his energy.

LEVI: Everything I did was focused around what I looked like, what people thought of me, what they were saying about me.

TERRY: He could encourage other people, but Levi troubled himself with lack of self-motivation. It was like that old mindset, "I'm fat. I'm slow. I'm not good," kind of still hung around even when Levi looked better. "I'm not very good. Why would somebody want me?"

He didn't know what to do with his life. He'd say, "Hey, I think I'll do this." He'd go down that road, and then say, "No, I don't want to do that. Maybe I'll try something else."

We really saw Levi drifting.

LEVI: And then one day I just got sick of it and I went to my mom and said, "Mom, this is what's going on. I think I need to see somebody, because this is controlling my life."

So I saw a therapist. A Christian lady our family knew. It became one of the turning points in my life.

I remember her asking me, "Levi, I want you to think about everything that makes you insecure. Think about these things you're struggling with. Close your eyes when you think about them, and lift your arms up to your side, and don't allow me to press down on your arms. I'm going to try my hardest, but don't let me press your arms down."

"Okay," I said.

Now, this lady was small, and I was pretty strong. I closed my eyes and started thinking about these things. When she pressed down on my arms it felt like I had 100 pounds of weight pushing against me. My right arm went completely down to my side. I couldn't move it.

She said, "Okay, now I want you to think about the blessings in your life. Think about what is good, what fills you up, what brings you joy. Close your eyes again and don't let me press down."

So I did that. And when I opened my eyes, I saw this lady was hanging on for dear life to my arm, which I'd miraculously elevated.

I couldn't believe it! That was when I realized, "Okay, my mindset has to change. I have to begin to speak life over myself. I can't see myself for who I was or who I think I am. I have to see myself for who I truly am."

_____

TERRY: That was a pivotal thing, for Levi. He began working to overcome his insecurities.

_____

LEVI: Because of my insecurities I had become someone who started things, but I couldn't finish things. I didn't have the confidence to be a finisher. I was just a starter. That led to me getting bad grades. By my senior year, I ended up needing to take a full year of extra credits, plus another full year of credits on top of that online, just to graduate.

_____

TERRY: That was one of the hardest things for Nancy and me. We saw this kid with so much potential. You'd look at Levi and think he could do anything. But he didn't believe that.

_____

LEVI: I had teachers telling me, "You're not going to graduate, why are you even trying? There's no way you will!" Yada yada yada. All this negative stuff.

I ended up passing all my classes. In fact, I passed my last class at 11:30 at night, the night before graduation. And I was able to graduate.

_____

TERRY: Levi needed to fulfill a math class, an algebra class, that he was taking online. He'd failed the final a couple of times. It was late at night, Levi was in our kitchen. He looked at me and seemed defeated.

"I can't do it," he said. "I'm not gonna graduate."

I looked him straight in the eye and said, "Bud, here's the deal. You can do whatever you want, but you have to decide right now.

Are you going to graduate or not? If you're not, you're done. But if you are, you need to keep going."

He bowed his head and said, "I'm gonna do it."

And he did. He took the final at 11:30 the night before graduation. And he passed his last class.

LEVI: My whole senior year was like having that *a-ha* kind of moment. I realized my insecurities had so much power over me. I was beginning to take ownership of my life.

That was when the shift began. After high school, I really went through some ups and downs. I experienced the highs of feeling confident, and doing well in school, to the lows of feeling, "Man, I'm back in this borderline depressed state, I'm insecure, and not doing well in school."

TERRY: Levi's a dreamer. Graduating high school had a short-term effect. He still struggled with that old mindset.

He had a hard time following through. There was always a reason, there was always an excuse why Levi couldn't move forward.

LEVI: It was always something else or someone else.

TERRY: That was our struggle, as parents. I felt like a failure, because I wasn't able to help my son other than just supporting him. We still believed in Levi. We tried to help him find a direction for his future.

Levi was always thinking he had to choose a job. He was like, "Do I become a physical therapist? A firefighter? An accountant?"

LEVI: At one point I think I said, "I met an accountant, they're doing really well financially. I think maybe that's what I should do."

TERRY: I knew Levi wasn't wired to be an accountant, but all Nancy and I could do was remain patient, plant the seed, and try to guide him. "Levi, what makes you most alive? When are you the happiest? What are you doing that makes you feel fulfilled?" We tried to keep him moving down a path that allowed Levi's calling to become clearer for him.

These were trying times.

A lot of patience and a lot of prayer went into these times.

LEVI: Honestly, that's really when the Lord began to do work in my life. He kept reminding me that my confidence was never in Him, my security was never in Him, it was in, "Am I looking good? Am I feeling good? Am I performing well?" It was never in *Him.*

Throughout the next couple of years, I kept trying to find my identity. My identity at this point was fitness. It was my grades in college. It was making friends, being popular, which ultimately led to a dead end. My confidence and all my hope and ambition was in material things. But the Lord really got ahold of me in 2011 through a series of events.

I gained some weight back. That really demoralized me. I realized I didn't really have any friends around me, I was lonely, and I found myself in a depressed point. I ended up moving back home to Coeur d'Alene. There, over the course of a couple of years, the Lord kept peeling back the layers, stripping away the old me. Helping me see with crystal clarity why I kept coming back to this constant state of insecurity. Revealing to me that I was trying to find my identity in things other than Him.

It was in this moment of clarity when I thought, *I have to challenge myself, to see what I'm really capable of.*

I need a transformation.

I need one more chance.

That's what led up to Ironman.

CHAPTER THREE

Ironman Dreams

LEVI: I had seen the Ironman competition for years and years in town. It inspired me. But I never thought it would be something I could do.

I was still seeking a purpose for my life. I was 23 years old, not working at the time, living at my parents' home. I had no direction.

But I had grown a lot in my faith and was committed to moving forward in my life. I had gone through a period of disappointment, doubt, and painful self-examination. I was finally taking ownership of this season of change, of transformation.

I remember the day I decided to do Ironman. It was May 30, 2013.

I had a friend competing in the Coeur d'Alene Ironman that year. I was out for a jog that morning. While I was running, and doing some self-examination, something just hit me—this intense, overpowering feeling. I thought, *I've acknowledged where I'm at, I've acknowledged the need to grow in every area of my life, now what am I going to do about it?* That's when I realized: *It's up to me. I need to move forward. I need a change.*

For whatever reason, I had this crazy idea to compete in an Ironman triathlon.

Now, I had never done any sort of triathlon or endurance race before, but I knew that I needed to dedicate a year of my life to growing in every area. I decided to compete in the next year's Ironman.

It would take a year of my life, challenge me in every area, force me to manage my time, and cause me to be more disciplined.

It would get me in better physical shape.

It would make me mentally stronger.

It would take *all* of me.

It would challenge me in every aspect of my life: spiritually, physically, mentally and emotionally. At the end of it, I wanted to be able to look back and say, "I am a completely different person than I was a year ago!"

Just thinking about those words—"I'm going to do an Ironman"—gave me a fresh excitement and passion.

TERRY: We all face tests. You can't be afraid to make mistakes. Mistakes are just the stepping-stones to success.

LEVI: I knew I would face doubters. I knew people would say, "Can Levi stick it out?" I knew I had always struggled with following through with my commitments.

For one thing, I had never run more than four miles.

I'd never been a cyclist, other than riding my little BMX bike.

I had never swum competitively or for distance.

Yet, for whatever reason, I decided, "I'm going to do an Ironman."

And in my own heart and in my own head I committed to it, that day. Ultimately, I made the commitment between myself and the Lord. No giving up on my goal. No distractions. No excuses. No *anything*—just one year of my life fully and passionately devoted to growing in every aspect. I knew training for an Ironman would take everything I had. I was focused, determined, and ready for a change.

TERRY: We could see something was happening in Levi's life. He suddenly seemed to be on a new path. He seemed happier. It was like he'd started to believe that change was possible.

LEVI: I remember the day I told a few friends and my parents. They were supportive. "Man, Levi, that's so cool!" they told me. "Good luck, you'll do great!" But deep inside, I knew no one believed I would actually do it.

TERRY: We didn't talk about this as a family, but none of us believed he would finish. It hurts to even say that but it is honestly how we felt. We had seen Levi's pattern. He'd get excited, he'd start something, then he wouldn't follow through. There was always an excuse.

LEVI: That didn't bother me. At that point, I had a lot to prove to myself. I knew my entire life I was a starter, not a finisher. I made excuses. I had a victim mindset: when things would happen to me, I always blamed others.

TERRY: We said, "Wow Bud, that's great. Good for you. We support you." We didn't think Levi would actually go through with it, even as the event got closer.

LEVI: Right off the bat, I could tell it was one of those things where it was all on me to get up every morning and start training. Right away, I set up meetings with friends who had competed in Ironman in the past to ask them questions. I knew I had a lot to learn and that in order to become a good triathlete, I needed to become a student of others and the sport.

I started saving money for a bike. Now, I'd never been good at saving money. But I saved $1000 in a couple months and bought my first bike to start training.

TERRY: As soon as Levi started training, you could see he was a completely different person.

Still, it was like there was a big question mark looming over him.

The truth is, Levi never had a swimming lesson in his life. He didn't own a bike. The furthest he'd ever run in his life was three or four miles.

He'd never been a guy to say, "I'm gonna do this," and then stick with it. The discipline he'd need to give himself over to, we'd never seen that. We didn't know if that was in him.

LEVI: The first thing I did after I signed up for Ironman was make it official on Facebook. I did that for accountability. I wanted to be held accountable to myself and my friends and family to my goals. I was determined to endure anything and to finish the race. There's a passage in the Bible, Hebrews 12:1-3, that talks about running your race. That verse became foundational for me during this season of my life.

I was in with both feet now. I was committed. Ready or not, I started training.

I remember my first official training run. I ran one mile from my home. I got one mile out and I couldn't even run anymore, I had to walk. I was wheezing, and gasping, and I needed my inhaler. I had to turn around, and walk all the way home.

Then the first time I trained for the swim . . . Honestly, I swam 50 yards and just got exhausted, I was ready to drop, burned out, because I had never done it before. I didn't have the stamina. I didn't have the breathing down. I didn't know what I was doing at all.

That's when it hit me, how much work I had to do. I realized, "Man, I've never swum! I'm not a good runner. I ran one mile and I'm exhausted and I have to do a 140.6-mile triathlon?!"

My good friend Sam, who is a two-time Ironman and a great swimmer, worked with me on my swimming. Sam told me I was a natural in the water, and just need to focus on technique, which gave me a lot of confidence!

The first six months of training were spent getting the basics down and developing a solid foundation. My official training plan started in February 2014, after I had moved to Kirkland, Washington for school.

During training, I decided again that I wasn't going to let myself get sidetracked. I stayed focused. I decided I wasn't going to date, and I knew I probably wasn't going to have much of a social life. I was committed to serving God and working every day toward my goals.

It was during my training that I met my future wife, Sarah. We met in the same chapel that my mom and dad met in, at the same college, at Northwest University.

I had a secret crush on Sarah. I ended up telling my parents, "Hey, I saw this beautiful girl in chapel, there's just something about her." Of course I knew their story, that's where my dad met my mom and saw her for the first time, and my dad said, "Dude, you should talk to her."

TERRY: Nancy and I told Levi he should talk to Sarah and he laughed and said, "No, no way! She doesn't even know I exist!"

LEVI: A week later, I was serving at a restaurant, The Keg Steakhouse and Bar, in Kirkland. Sarah came in with a friend and sat in my section. I was nervous, and I knew that she didn't know who I was so I decided to play dumb. I pretended that she looked familiar, and asked her if she went to Northwest University. She said yes, and I told her that I thought I had a class with her. She had no idea I knew who she was and had a secret crush on her.

It was kind of funny. Sarah didn't say much. Her friend was the talkative one. But as the night went on, we had a chance to get to know each other. And from the moment I met Sarah, I knew there was something special about her.

On our first "date," Sarah asked me, "What are your intentions with me?" The question caught me off-guard, but I was glad she asked it. I replied, "When I asked you if you would go to lunch with me, I said that I wanted to get to know you better. From what I know, you're an amazing girl, but I am just starting to know you. So, as of now, my intentions are to continue to get to know you better."

Sarah told me she wasn't ready to be in a relationship, but would like to get to know me better, too. Which worked out perfectly, since I'd made the commitment not to date until the end of June. So Sarah and I continued to spend time together, and get to know each other. We ended up becoming good friends, and decided to grow our friendship during that season.

As much as I liked Sarah, I was thankful we decided to become friends first, before dating. That helped me stay committed to my training and transformation.

TERRY: Levi was living in Kirkland, and doing his training over there. We never saw him train. He'd call us in the morning, the phone would ring at 7 AM, which was early for him.

"Hey Mom and Dad, what are you doing?"

"We're just sitting here having coffee, Levi, what are you doing?"

"Oh, I just got done with a swim."

Nancy and I would fist-bump each other and say, "He's doing it!"

LEVI: Even though I was training and growing, I still battled insecurity and doubt at times. I'd find myself thinking, "Who am I kidding? Can I actually *do this?*"

There were times I felt alone, even though I had a lot of support.

My good friend Luke was always checking in with me. He'd call me once a week, and coach me up. Luke believed I would do it. Every time we talked he would encourage me, tell me that I'm doing great, and tell me that I'm going to be an Ironman.

Luke is also a two-time Ironman and a freak of an athlete. So when he would give me advice and encouragement, I listened!

"You see what you accomplished this week?" Luke always challenged me. "You're doing great! Keep it up! Right now, you're a Tin Man, but soon you'll be an Ironman!"

TERRY: In the past, Levi had bought into disappointment. Now Levi had totally bought into his future.

LEVI: I trained hard every day. I'd get up at 4:30, 5:00 AM, and either go to the pool, go for a run, or go for a bike ride.

I was getting better each day in all three disciplines. I was becoming a good swimmer by consistently focusing on technique, breathing and spending a lot of time in the pool. I was becoming a better cyclist by putting in hours on my bike trainer and hundreds of miles on the road. And I learned to love running. Running was something that always intimidated me and was always hard for me, but I was learning to love it and getting better each day.

I was taking 17 credits at school, working 20 hours a week at my job, while at the same time training for an Ironman.

I learned to be disciplined, because I had to. I learned to time-manage, because I had to. I learned to take ownership if I missed a workout or I woke up late. It wasn't someone else's fault, it was my fault. I had grown a lot! Spiritually, I was a new man.

Physically, I had gotten in the best shape of my life. Mentally, I was tougher than ever.

I was ready to finish what I'd started.

TERRY: A month before the race, we finally saw Levi. He came back home, and he looked great. He looked *fantastic*. Better than he's ever looked. I was really proud of that. I was like, "Wow. This is impressive."

LEVI: I did six months of my training over in the Seattle area. I ended up coming back home a month before Ironman to finish training and get myself ready for the race.

I had a group of friends in Coeur d'Alene who were also doing Ironman, so we spent the last month training together. That last month leading up to the race consisted of many hours and hundreds of miles training. We spent that time training on the actual Ironman course, which was great for me since I hadn't done much training in Coeur d'Alene. We trained hard and consistently all the way up until race week.

Race week was amazing. Family and friends had come to town to support me. The energy in the air was unlike anything I'd ever experienced. I'd trained for an entire year for this day. I'd devoted and dedicated this season of my life for this moment. I was prepared and equipped to reach the finish line of the Ironman and of this season.

The night before the race came. We had this big, celebratory family meal. Chicken, potatoes, and white rice. I was chowing down on carbs and protein. I had to get up at 3:00 in the morning, so at 7:30 that night, right before I went to bed, my friends and family circled around me, and prayed for me.

TERRY: We prayed about Levi's race. We prayed over his future, that God would sustain him to reach his goals.

LEVI: I knew there was still a part of my dad that didn't believe I would do it. He pulled me aside and said, "Bud, I just want you to know I'm so proud of you. You look great, you've worked really hard, and I just want you to know that even if you don't finish, you have nothing to be ashamed of."

I remember just looking at him—not in a bothered way, but almost fired up, you know? I told him, "Dad, not finishing is not an option. That won't happen. It's a matter of whether I get the time I want or not."

TERRY: Levi not finishing was *my* expectation. Shame on me. Right? That was my expectation, based on the past.

But Levi telling me that *not* finishing wasn't an option . . . that was the first time I'd ever heard my son speak with that kind of focus, that kind of confidence. I thought, *Wow. Okay. All right, man. Let's do it.*

CHAPTER FOUR

Levi and the First Ironman

LEVI: The next morning I woke at 3. It's race morning, the house is all lit up, my friends and family are all there and my dad is making me breakfast.

I arrived at the Ironman Village by 4:30. We parked by the lake, and the first thing I noticed was the weather. Chilly. And windy. *Very* windy. The wind was creating some serious waves in the lake. *Man,* I thought to myself, *this is gonna be rough. I've never swum in water this rough.* Headwind on a bike is the worst, so I was a little worried about the bike too, but I felt confident. I was not even going to concern myself with the wind.

I had a lot of things going through my mind.

I thought about how far I'd come, to reach this moment.

I thought about Sarah.

I thought about my family and friends who were supporting me.

Just a year ago, I'd been in a totally different place. Now I was about to compete in an Ironman race, the very thing I'd spent a year training for.

I thought about that, as I lined up on the beach, and prepared to start the race.

TERRY: We're watching and waiting for the race to start. There are 2,000 Ironman competitors lined up on the beach, and somewhere in the midst of them is Levi. My stomach is killing me. I'm not kidding. Nancy and I, our stomachs are hurting because Levi was about to be in the water with 2,000 other athletes and because we weren't there to see him train, we still didn't know how strong of a swimmer he was.

LEVI: I'm standing on the beach, with thousands of other athletes, thinking, *Holy smokes, this is it.*

Then the gun sounds.

The race starts.

I rush off. Getting closer and closer to the water. *Man, I'm actually doing this!* I'm thinking, *I know I can do this, I have a long day ahead of me, so take it one step at a time.*

The swim is two loops. Each loop is 1.2 miles. I focused on one loop at a time.

Believe me, there's nothing in the world like being in the water with thousands of people. Athletes swimming over you, under you, kicking you . . . it's insane! And I loved it! It was inspiring, being in the water with that many people with the same goal in mind, to be an Ironman.

I'm swimming and focusing on my technique and breathing, trying to avoid getting kicked in the face by other competitors. I'm timing my strokes so I can breathe and focusing on one stroke at a time.

I noticed a lot of people were panicking, getting scared and freaking out with the swim. Not me. I enjoyed it. I completed my first loop, and then jumped back into the water to begin my second loop. I'd hit a good rhythm and was feeling great! As I approached the end of the swim, I experienced this feeling of joy. Intense joy.

I did it.

This is one of the three phases. I'm about to be done. I'm about to get on my bike.

Amazing!

TERRY: I'm feeling sick. I mean *really* sick. I didn't know if I could stand up. People are swimming, and I don't know where Levi's at. Everybody looks the same.

They finish their first loop. Then the second. I'm a nervous wreck. And then someone says, "Here he comes!"

Levi comes out of the water, dripping wet.

We didn't know what he was going to look like. If he was going to be exhausted and tired or need to be dragged out of the lake. We just didn't know.

He came running up. He had this big smile. It was like, "Wow."

My heart stopped. We expected to see him struggling, gasping and wheezing and losing that Ironman intensity and beginning to dial it down.

But that isn't what we saw. We saw our son kicking butt. We saw a young man prepared to overcome anything that stood in the path to his dreams.

LEVI: I was so fired-up when I got out of the water! I made a good transition from the swim to the bike and was ready to crush this 112-mile ride!

I started out strong on the bike, feeling good and riding at a solid pace. My first 56-mile loop was great! 112 miles is a long distance to ride though, especially on a hilly course like Coeur d'Alene. It was windy . . . *really* windy. I hadn't really trained on many rides in the wind, so a lot of it was just mindset, trying to control my mind, staying in the present. Reminding myself I trained for this, and spending a lot of time praying.

Throughout the ride, I ended up passing people and riding next to people who were super-encouraging. Everyone was like, "Hey, good job! Looking good!"

TERRY: Every time we saw him, on the bike course, we'd hold up our signs and yell. As he passed, I'm leaning in and trying to get locked in on Levi's eyes, because the eyes tell us so much. I tried to see if his eyes were telling me that he's hurting, that he's questioning if he can make it, or if he's determined.

Every single time, Levi was focused and determined. Every time he saw us, he would give us the "hang loose" sign and this big smile. Like he was really enjoying this.

LEVI: One thing I heard a lady say before the race, that really stuck with me, was, "Smile every mile." My goal was to keep a smile on my face the whole way. If I could be an encouragement to somebody else, that was what I wanted.

I knew it wasn't just about me. It was about all of us finishing this race.

The bike ride was intense. It was 45 minutes longer than I had trained for because the wind was so strong.

For about half the ride it was in my face. It was like I was riding with a parachute on the back of my bike.

It was seven hours and ten minutes on the bike—just staying focused, staying in the moment, not getting discouraged. And then you still need to run a marathon!

TERRY: It's brutal. But each loop around the course, Levi got to see his family and everyone who was cheering him on. So that helped a ton.

LEVI: I looked forward to going through town and seeing my family. Just to get the extra little boost. That bit of encouragement and motivation.

When I got off my bike, my whole family was there, waiting at the transition to the run, cheering me on and asking how I was feeling. Honestly, I was feeling *amazing*. I had trained well for the race. Obviously I was tired, but I was conditioned and feeling great. Getting off the bike and onto the run was an incredible feeling, because I realized, "Man, this is the last leg of my race!"

TERRY: Levi came out of the transition. We were standing by the fence where the cyclists exited. Levi came out and hugged his mom. He looked great. It didn't look like he had just finished a 112-mile bike ride!

"Bud," I asked him, "how do you feel?"

He smiled. "Dad, I feel really good. I'm ready to run."

I smiled. I'd never felt so relieved in my entire life. Then off he went on the run.

LEVI: At that point, I knew. I had made it. It was just a matter of finishing strong.

My whole run, I paced myself, running with different people, just chatting with them, hearing about their journey.

TERRY: We saw Levi at the halfway point, the 13.1 mile mark. He took some sodium and told us how good he was feeling.

LEVI: There was a lot of joy and energy on the run. I would tear up, just thinking about the last year and how much growth had taken place in my life. I was filled with so much gratitude for this transformative season of my life, and began to get a glimpse of what crossing this finish line would symbolize: the end of one season, and the beginning of another.

As I ran I counted down. Six miles to go. Five miles. Then four. Then three . . .

By the time I'd made it back into town, I had run 26 exhausting miles and was a quarter mile away from the finish. Experienced tri-athletes who had prepared me for the race recalled the surrealness of this moment. At this point, it's a straight shot to the finish line, as crowds of supporters cheer you on with cowbells and cheering. I approached Sherman Avenue, finding it difficult to hide the emotion welling up inside.

TERRY: A family friend, Dave Miller, saw Levi coming toward Sherman. Dave rushed out and gave Levi a big bear-hug and told him, "You're gonna do it!" Then Dave texted us: *Here he comes!*

LEVI: When I turned onto Sherman and I saw that finish line, I just teared up. I was so emotional. I had a huge smile on my face. It was unlike anything I'd ever experienced before. At that moment, it all became real to me. It was the most amazing feeling of accomplishment and I was truly proud of myself.

I'm about to finish an Ironman! Something I never really thought I'd ever be able to do. Something I never would have envisioned myself doing before, so it was a powerful, emotional moment.

TERRY: We waited by the finish line. Looking and looking and looking. *Where's Levi?*

Finally, we could see him. He got closer and entered the finisher's chute. He was running flat-out. And he had this big, huge Levi smile on his face.

LEVI: There was this amazing, just beautiful sunset that day. I was heading toward the finish line right at sunset and it was gorgeous. I had this thought that the sun is setting on this season of my life.

TERRY: We're waiting at the finish line and we're yelling at the top of our lungs. "Levi, Levi!"

Finally Levi stopped when he was two feet away from crossing the finish line. That's when he heard us. He ran over and we all high-fived. Tears were running down my face. All at once, we heard Mike Riley, the announcer, over the loudspeaker: "Levi Gurno from Coeur d'Alene, Idaho—*you are an Ironman!*"

LEVI: My whole family was cheering, yelling, screaming, snapping pictures. Part of me didn't want the race to be over. I wanted to *keep going.*

I remember my dad hugging me and telling me, "Less than 0.01% of the world's population will ever finish an Ironman. Levi, you're in that 0.01% in the world!"

I'd made a promise to myself: that I was going to give my best on every single step of this entire race.

You know, I really did. *I did it.*

I finished in 14 hours and 9 minutes.

And now, I was an Ironman!

CHAPTER FIVE

The Aftermath: Terry's Challenge

TERRY: I've always had excuses and fears and doubts that have held me back and buried my dreams. But seeing Levi overcome the Ironman wakened something.

It was inspiring.

Years before, after watching my first Coeur d'Alene Ironman, I thought, *I want to do this*. I didn't tell anybody. I just started thinking and dreaming about it.

The more I thought about it, the more my thoughts killed the dream. "You know what? I could never do this. What am I thinking? I could never learn to swim."

Every year, that's the way I felt. Ironman would come to town, and I'd think, "I'd love to do this. But I could never swim. And my knees are bad, I could never do the marathon."

A high percentage of people in the stands are thinking the same thing. "You know what? I think I could do everything but the swim, I could never do the swim." Or, "112 miles on a bike would kill me."

That's exactly what I thought, too.

LEVI: The day after my race, my parents went with me to the Ironman finisher's breakfast. My dad kept telling me how watching me finish the race had changed his life. It was a life-changing thing for my whole family and so the next day my dad's still talking about that, talking about how amazing it was and how I'd transformed my life on every level with my physical and spiritual overhaul. "It's one of the most awe-inspiring life-transformations ever!" he'd say, with this proud look in his eyes.

We're driving home and he's still talking about it! "Man, I can't get over it! Levi, I'm so proud of you! I've always wanted to do an Ironman," he kept insisting, and pounding on the steering wheel, "but there's no way I could."

TERRY: There were moments where I was on the verge, after each Ironman, thinking, "I'm gonna do it. This year, I'm gonna sign up." Then I'd walk from the finish line back to my car to go home and I would think, *No you're not, Gurno. There's just no way you could ever do it.*

The thing is, I was so inspired by Levi! It was the next day in my truck that I was telling him how awesome his race was, how inspiring, and how proud I was as his father.

"You know," I blurted out, "I've always wanted to do the Ironman." I kept going on and on, telling him how much I loved this and was inspired by that.

Levi just looked at me.

"Dad, what did you say?"

I said, "I loved that moment when—"

"No, Dad, before that?" I could see his face was radiating shock.

I hesitated. "That I've always wanted to do the Ironman?"

"Yeah," Levi said.

Out of the corner of my eye, I could see this sudden realization hit Levi. I could almost see the gears churning in his head.

"You know," I answered, in a resigned voice, "I've thought about it." I shrugged. "But the truth is, I could never do it."

LEVI: I sat there, wondering why he was making all these excuses about something that meant so much to him.

"Well, you know," he said, "I have bad knees. I'm overweight. I just couldn't do it."

Honestly, he was just giving me all these lame excuses. It was like he was locked into this limiting belief, like he truly believed that this dream of his wasn't possible.

So I did what my dad had always done for me. I coached him up, and I said, "Why do you feel that way?"

TERRY: I reacted with instant fear. I started thinking hard and fast. "Well, for one thing," I explained, "I could never learn to swim."

"Well, Dad," Levi said, "you can learn to swim if you start swimming. I didn't swim a year ago. You can learn to swim if you start."

"Yeah, well that may be true," I shot back.

Levi smiled. "It's not that it *may* be true, Dad. It *is* true."

See, here's the deal. Levi was trying to break down this wall I'd created. He was systematically removing my excuses. Isolating the reason, the challenges, and erasing all my excuses.

I said, "Yeah, but here's the deal, Bud. I have arthritis and bone spurs in my knees." This is true. If I stand for a couple of hours at a time, my knees swell. They can barely bend. Running a marathon sounded crazy! I told Levi, "Bud, that's never happening."

Levi smiled and nodded. "Well, here's the deal, Dad. You're going to lose weight when you're swimming and riding your bike so it'll be easier on your knees." Shooting down every one of my excuses.

LEVI: He said, "You know I can't swim. I don't know how to swim." And I told him, "Listen, Dad, it was the same for me. I didn't know how to swim. But if you start, you can learn. All you gotta do is start."

TERRY: He said, "The truth is, Dad, you might not be able to run a marathon. But you can walk it. And you can make it."

LEVI: I challenged my dad. He'd preached this same thing to me my whole life. It was literally just a father and a son having a conversation, but I could tell this was something he wanted to do and was making excuses.

After he was done giving me all the excuses he could give me, I knew they weren't valid, because I was in the same boat a year before. Finally, I asked him, "Dad, do you want to do it, or *not?*"

TERRY: Levi's "Do you want to do it or not?" question stunned me. My immediate reaction was a surge of adrenaline. I knew the answer. But I was too scared to give him the answer. It scared me to say it. It frustrated me to be in that moment where my son is asking me the question that really needs to be asked. I was agitated.

Levi repeated, "Do you want to do it, Dad? Or not? Yes or no? That's the bottom line."

There was really no point in him asking the question. He knew the answer. I felt this huge smile spread across my face. I looked at him and I said, "Yes!" I clenched my fists, finally ready to face my demons, and said "Yes!" again.

"Okay," Levi said, meeting my adrenaline rush with a smile. "But Dad listen: if you're going to do it, then I'm going to do it with you."

I felt my hands trembling. "No way, Levi, you can't do this again! You put your life on hold for an entire year to do this race. I would never expect you to do this again."

"That doesn't matter!" Levi responded, "I loved it! And if you're going to do it, I'm going to do it with you!"

Then came the terrifying call to action. Levi said, "Dad, a year from today, you're going to be an Ironman"

Man, that was powerful!

When Levi said that, something filled me with awe. My soul was ignited. I had pushed that old buried dream down and felt resigned that it would never, ever happen.

"Okay," I told him, my voice shaking in expectation of the inevitable reality check. "But we're not telling Mom!" I didn't think Nancy would be too excited about it.

LEVI: I'd decided during the conversation that if my dad said he was going for it, then I was going to do it with him. I wanted to be there for him and experience that dream with my dad. So we made the decision right then and there.

This was going to be our goal.

We would move forward.

We'd break down walls. We'd redefine what's possible.

A year from that day, I was going to be a two-time Ironman. And my dad was going to be an Ironman, too.

TERRY: We sealed the deal with a hug and a high-five. We were both *in!* Immediately this foreboding thought crept into my panicked mind:

Gurno, what have you gotten yourself into?

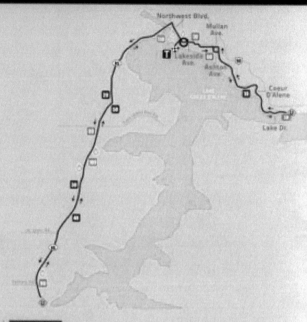

TURN BY TURN DIRECTIONS

- Exit transition
- Turn right on Northwest Boulevard
- Left on Lakeside Avenue
- Right on 8th Street
- Left on Sherman Avenue
- Right on 11th Street
- Left on Mullan Avenue
- Right on 23rd Street
- Left on Ashton Avenue
- Right on Coeur D'Alene Lake Drive
- Turnaround at the Higginspoint cul de sac
- Left on Mullan Avenue
- Right on 11th Street
- Left on Sherman Avenue
- Right on 8th Street
- Left on Lakeside Avenue
- Right on Northwest Boulevard
- Right on US-95 Ramp
- Left on US-95
- Continue south on Northwest Boulevard
- Repeat loop
- After second loop, turn right on Mullan Avenue
- Finish at City Park Transition Area

LEGEND

- TRANSITION AREA
- START LINE
- FINISH LINE
- 1ˢᵗ LOOP MILE MARKERS
- 2ⁿᵈ LOOP MILE MARKERS
- SPECIAL NEEDS
- BEGIN 2ⁿᵈ LOOP
- U-TURN
- WATER/AID STATION

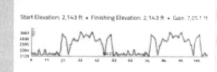

Start Elevation: 2,143 ft • Finishing Elevation: 2,143 ft • Gain: 7,051 ft

PART TWO

THE DEATH OF THE DREAM

CHAPTER SIX

The Journey to 140.6

TERRY: From that moment Levi became my mentor and coach. It was such an incredible thing to see him leading me down this path. For that year, he really led me.

"Dad, here's what we have to do . . . Dad, here's your training schedule . . . Dad, keep thinking about this . . . Dad, stay focused on that."

It was like the dad taking care of his son, but it was really the son taking care of his dad. It was like that the entire year.

LEVI: He says I became his mentor. A lot of it was just sit-down conversations about, "Hey, Dad, here's what to expect. Here's what we need to start working on right now. Clean up your diet. Get used to exercising five days a week."

I went through the plan to prep for Ironman together. It was a twenty-week plan that would start in February. I was committed to getting him to a point where he could do the workout and the plan by himself, since I was living on the other side of the state. So I guess you could say I was mentoring him in that.

———

TERRY: Levi was living in Kirkland, so we didn't get to workout a lot together. When I was in the Seattle area we would swim together or we'd bike together.

Levi was such an encourager. He would say, "Dad, you're doing great, you're coming so far!" We talked a lot, because I trained here and he trained there. He would ask me how my training was going because we followed the same schedule.

———

LEVI: He already had a bike, and so starting out it was really just getting in shape. It was, "Hey let's go to the gym together!" "Hey, let's go on a ride!" We were developing a base.

———

TERRY: One day, I was swimming and I was really discouraged in my swim. Discouraged because I'd arrived there early and watched people swim. I would look at this guy tearing up the pool and go, "Wow, that was fast!" I'd time that person, see how fast they were going.

Then I'd look at people who were slow. I mean like *really* slow. I'd watch them and think to myself, *Wow. I can't possibly be that slow.* Then I got in the water and started timing myself. I was slower than the slowest person I had watched.

I was really, *really* discouraged.

I remember Levi called and he said, "Dad, how was your swim?"

I said, "You know Bud, it was okay, but I'm pretty discouraged."

He said, "Dad, why are you discouraged?"

I told him. Levi said, "Dad, why are you watching other people? Why does that matter? Why does how fast they're swimming matter to you when this is *your* race?"

LEVI: He was just really bummed. I told him, "You know, Dad, that's okay. You don't need to worry about the guy to your right, the guy to your left. You need to worry about *you*. Swim in your lane and stay focused."

At the end of the day, you're not running someone else's race. You're running your race.

TERRY: That was exactly what I needed to hear. I wasn't focused on what I was doing. I had to find a way to tune that out.

To say I was discouraged is an understatement. But Levi picked me up. It's important to have that somebody who's cheering for you and committed to you.

LEVI: I just encouraged him to focus all his time, energy and effort on *his* swim. Sure enough, a month later, he had cut four seconds off a lap.

TERRY: Levi said, "Dad, don't watch anybody else. Focus on what you can do to get better. This is all about *your* race, for *your* reasons. Don't look at anybody else."

Then we would go on bike rides together. We'd start at the same time, but we were rarely together because Levi was so much faster than me and so we'd be riding and I wouldn't see him for 15 or 20 minutes, a half an hour. Then all of a sudden, here he comes, he's coming my way, coming back just to make sure I'm okay.

"Are you okay, Dad?"

"Yep, I'm okay."

I mean this whole year, "Dad, are you okay? How are you doing, Dad?"

LEVI: We trained a lot together. We'd go on training rides, go swim at the pool, and go for runs. It was great because I was able to help coach him up before I moved back to Kirkland. We were apart for the bulk of our training. We'd text each other, every single morning. "Hey, are you up?" "Hey, just making sure you're awake and headed to the pool." Stuff like that. He had downloaded this running and cycling app called Strava. It enabled me to look at his workouts from afar and see, "Okay, looks like you struggled there, and it looks like you picked up the pace here."

Throughout this whole journey to prep for Ironman, I was sharing bits and pieces of everything I'd learned. The process. What to do. What not to do.

We knew we'd have six to eight weekends throughout the year where we'd be together. We made sure we got in at least one run, one ride, and one swim.

We capitalized on every weekend. When I say we talked on the phone every day, we did. I mean, every day was like, "Hey, how are you doing?" "Hey, in one year you're gonna be an Ironman." "In eight months, you're gonna be an Ironman." "In five months, you're gonna be an Ironman."

Every day, it was just encouraging each other, lifting each other up, getting pumped up, and just really being in it together. We stayed focused to conquer the 140.6. That was our goal.

CHAPTER SEVEN

Old Demons Popping Up

TERRY: The important thing to me was getting my mind right. Getting mentally prepared to compete in an Ironman. Completing Ironman wasn't just important to me—it was a *mission*. Yet, the whole time I'm training, I'm still not sure I can do it.

Can my body handle this? Can I withstand the pain? Will I find the courage to finish, to let go of my fears?

It's almost like being fear-driven, as opposed to confidence-driven. Because when you see the Ironman trucks roar into town, a week before the race, that's when you know.

It's *real*.

LEVI: We trained hard for this race. We were prepared. Physically prepared. But also mentally. We each had a goal in mind. Mine was to finish in under 13 hours. My dad's was to finish in under 17 hours, which is the Ironman cut-off time. We'd need real grit to accomplish these goals.

TERRY: I've often said: mindset is your beliefs, which determine your decisions, which determine your actions, which determine your results. You need to understand the power and the importance of mindset to be able to climb the mountain to your dreams without stopping.

LEVI: My dad always talked and talked to us kids about our mindset. Mindset was one of the biggest lessons I'd learned throughout my first Ironman. Ironman is just as much mental as it is physical.

TERRY: To be honest, I'm not convinced I really did conquer my mindset. The whole time I was preparing my body to complete an Ironman, my mind was realizing the magnitude of the challenge. There was still a big question mark hanging over me.

Why am I doing this to myself?

My denial was about to morph into my greatest fear: fear of failure. Of the dreaded DNF—Did Not Finish. Because that's when a couple of things happened.

I competed in a sprint triathlon in May, a month before Ironman. Now, I'd never done a triathlon. *Never.* But someone suggested I do it, just to see how it went.

It was the Troika, out at Medical Lake, in Eastern Washington. And even though I had trained to swim 2.4 miles at this point and I was only swimming 880 yards at the Troika, I was overwhelmed with panic. I'd heard that sometimes when you get in a large group of people in the water, you panic. You lose your nerve.

The day of the Troika came. I warmed up fine. I was in the water, with my fellow competitors, when the gun went off. But when the race started, it was like I couldn't move my legs, and all my training went out the window.

I panicked.

I started hyperventilating.

A wave of anxiety washed over me.

I couldn't swim. My mind froze. Every thought I had was, *I can't do this* and *I can't do that. Go home, Gurno, go home.*

Nancy, Chelsea and Ali had come to support me, and they could see from the shore that I was panicking. I'm sure they were thinking, *How on earth is he going to manage to complete a full-on Ironman?*

I didn't quit—although I almost did. I just did the breaststroke the whole way through the swim.

When I climbed out of the water, I was beat, I was exhausted. With all my rapid breathing I was ready to drop. I got on my bike. The bike part of the Troika was only 12 miles, but I hadn't even recovered from the swim yet, and I was even more dog-tired by the time I finished the 12-mile ride.

This really made me nervous. I thought, *What am I doing? This is just a sprint, just a 880-yard swim, and a 12-mile bike ride. I've got a 2.4-mile swim and 112-mile bike ride ahead of me, in a month!*

LEVI: I know that first triathlon messed with my dad. I could sense his distress. He felt way out of his league.

TERRY: But the Troika wasn't the only thing.

The year before, I'd biked from Seattle to Portland, Oregon. 204 miles, on a two-day ride.

The temperature hit 95 degrees the first day. At mile 113, I over-heated. I felt my heart rate go into the danger zone. I had to stop. It took me twenty minutes of drinking water and packing my shirt with ice to cool my body down. Then I kept going.

But at mile 140, my body just shut down and I was unable to go any further.

Nancy was waiting at our day one destination, seven miles away. The guy I was riding with called Nancy and said, "Listen, Terry's okay, but you need to get some ice and come get him."

By the time Nancy arrived—honestly I couldn't think, I couldn't even stand up, I was done. I had to be told what to do.

I'm sure that experience was on Nancy's mind, knowing the Coeur d'Alene Ironman was coming up in the sweltering days of June.

LEVI: A week before the Coeur d'Alene Ironman race, you could feel the excitement.

You could also feel the pressure building.

TERRY: The Ironman trucks are here, they're pulling into town. They're starting to set up the course and the signs are going up.

Inside my mind is racing with thoughts of *It's here!* At the same time, the fear is ramping up. It's becoming more and more real and more intensified. I began to struggle to stay on top of that with my mindset.

Not focusing on my fears became a lot of work.

I kept feeling overwhelmed. Instead, I focused my mind on what I *could* do. Levi said it would take mental and spiritual discipline to complete an Ironman. I was starting to understand what he meant.

No problem, I thought. *I've got this.*

Just when I felt like I had taken a great leap forward, the unthinkable happened.

In the days before the race, we started hearing the weather was going to be super-hot.

LEVI: We started watching the weather. We heard it was going to be 100 degrees. I knew the Troika race had heightened my dad's fears. I wasn't going to let our minds go there.

"Yeah, it's going to be hot," I told my dad. "But we prepared for this."

TERRY: I'd heard the weather reports. First it was going to be in the low 90s. Then it looked like it would be in the high 90s. Then I heard our friends talking: "Oh, it's going to be 100." "Wow, it looks like it's going to be 107."

I was super-aware. The heat was coming. The heat was going to be on.

I was legitimately concerned about it. Nancy was getting text messages from her friends: "Please, don't let Terry do this!" Nancy's not telling me, but Nancy's thinking the same thing. She's concerned.

Me? I was concerned, but I didn't share that with anyone. Why say that? Why speak into my fears? It's only going to make people worry.

Up to the day before, the race officials were talking about canceling that year's Ironman. What they decided was they'd start the race an hour early—which was great for the pros.

But it didn't make a bit of difference for somebody like me.

LEVI: We knew if it's hot, we'd have to stay on top of our nutrition. We'd have to make sure we're drinking enough water, and listening to our bodies. Regardless of the temperature, Ironman was never going to be easy. It's up to me to encourage my dad and up to my dad to encourage me.

Meanwhile, the week before Ironman was a week I'll never forget.

TERRY: We'd get up every morning and do a short workout.

LEVI: We mapped out our race, right down to the minute. Stuff like, when are we going to drink water? What else are we going to drink? What nutrition will we take? We were going to give it all we had, but we had to be smart, we had to be wise with our nutrition and listen to our bodies.

I remember soaking it all in. "Let's go to the Ironman Village. Let's go meet the other athletes. Let's do a practice swim, down at the lake. Let's do a run down by the Village."

We both prayed hard, because we didn't want the race to be cancelled. We'd trained all year for this. The night before, we found out the race was on, even with the extreme heat.

TERRY: I'd heard there were 400 athletes who decided not to do the race. They expected it to hit 86 degrees by six in the morning.

The day before was tense. That's when you go and check your bike in, and you can't touch it until the next morning. I recalled watching Levi take his bike in, the year before. Now here we were, doing that together.

It was a very cool moment, in an extremely tense time.

We also had to put together these bags, called transition bags, and special needs bags.

Each athlete has two transition bags. They contain everything you need to go on your bike. Your helmet, your gloves, your glasses, your shoes. That's your T-1 bag. The next bag, the T-2, is everything you need for the transition to running the marathon.

Then there's the special needs bags. There's a special needs bag for the bike, containing the things you want to have to eat and drink on your ride. There's another bag for running. So when we brought our bikes down, we also brought our transition bags.

It was inspiring. But it was also becoming scary. All the old demons I'd fought off, all these months, began popping up.

Look, I'm not a professional athlete. I'm not an Olympic swimmer, or a marathon runner. I'm just a middle-aged guy who wanted to compete in the Ironman, and face that challenge.

By this point, I wasn't worried about Levi. I knew Levi could handle himself. And I wasn't too worried about my mindset. I was more worried about my physical well-being. The last thing I wanted was to get to the same place I did on the Seattle-to-Portland race, to get to the point where my body seized up, where my lungs were screaming and I needed to stop.

To get to the point where I quit.

CHAPTER EIGHT

"Get a Good Night's Sleep . . . Seriously?"

TERRY: One of the hardest things was going to sleep the night before. The idea of competing in an Ironman the next day suddenly seemed all the more impossible.

LEVI: Did I get a good night's sleep? The night before Ironman?

Not only was I preparing to do an Ironman in 107-degree heat, but let me tell you a little secret.

I was proposing to my wife-to-be Sarah, the day after the race.

TERRY: The night before Ironman, we had a bunch of friends and family over. Sarah and her family were in town. We had friends coming up from California. Levi had friends there, and it was just a big party, it was a lot of fun.

We had dinner early that night, because we were planning on being in bed by 7:00. We all sat around the campfire we'd built, and sang songs. Then we prayed, and Levi and I said goodnight and climbed in bed.

It was still light outside, so we darkened our windows. The heat was suffocating. The house didn't have air conditioning, but we had a portable air conditioner in our room that night, so we could sleep in the heat.

LEVI: We had a ton of people staying at the house. So many, that I had to sleep on a blow-up mattress on my parents' floor. I already have trouble sleeping—I sleepwalk—and the night before the Ironman I ended up sleepwalking and jumping onto my parents' bed, thinking I was in the water.

TERRY: I kept waking up. Dozing off for a minute, and startling awake. In my dreams I ran and ran and ran. I woke, and lay there, sleepless, with the air conditioner chugging, thinking about all the people who would be disappointed if I failed.

LEVI: At the same time, we had planned for not sleeping well that night. You don't expect to get a good night's sleep the night before pushing your body to its limits in a 140.6-mile triathlon. That just doesn't happen.

TERRY: I tossed and turned, and got as much sleep as I could. It was hard to sleep because we were getting up at 3:00 in the morning. I don't know if we got two hours of sleep that night.

LEVI: I was lying in bed, in the heat, thinking about it being my engagement week. Sarah's whole family would be there, when I proposed. I felt nervous and excited thinking about that. Every time sleep started to sink in, my eyes would open. I could hear the house creaking. Our family talking. The next-door neighbors laughing. I'd wonder if my dad had fallen asleep, as I lay awake, my mind spinning.

TERRY: All I had to do was get up at three in the morning to swim 2.4 miles, bike 112 miles, and run a 26.2-mile marathon, all on a 100-degree day.

Get a good night's sleep? Before the biggest challenge of your life? Seriously??

CHAPTER NINE

Facing the Ironman

TERRY: Three o'clock came early. It was pitch black. The alarm clock went off. I gasped in a breath, and immediately remembered it was race day.

LEVI: My mind was fuzzy. I lay there awake, staring at the ceiling. Then I sat up, and ran my eyes around the dark room. I staggered off the blow-up mattress and headed downstairs to get ready.

TERRY: I felt anxious, but not panicked. Instantly I turned my attention to getting ready.

Levi had been blasting music all week long. There was one song he played, called "Hall of Fame," about achieving your goals. We were just cranking that, over and over.

LEVI: We were cranking that song while we were getting dressed and making breakfast. We were focused, anxious, excited, nervous, and trying to enjoy every minute of it.

TERRY: I did a check of our provisions for the day. Making sure we had everything we needed. Levi and I planned to eat a little bit more on the morning of the race, so we did.

LEVI: Our special pre-race ritual meal. Protein pancakes with almond butter and banana with egg whites. We gave each other pep talks and pumped each other up.

TERRY: We chowed down our breakfast. Made sure we double-checked our gear bags.

Soon it was time to go.

That's when it really started hitting me. There was no turning back.

LEVI: We climbed in my dad's truck. My dad and me, along with Sarah and her sister. The rest of our family was meeting us down there.

TERRY: We drove down to the race course. Everything was dark and silent, except for the purring of the engine. I was excited, inspired, letting my mind drift through my thoughts.

LEVI: The drive down was filled with a "quiet energy." We had some music on, but we were just focused. As we got closer to the race course, I looked at my dad. "Today's the day. We've got to lock it in. Make sure we're keeping up on our nutrition. It's going to be hot. But this is what we trained for."

TERRY: The first thing we did when we arrived at Ironman was get our bodies marked. That's where they write your number on both arms and your age on your left calf, with black markers. Then we went into where our bikes were parked, and started to get out our stuff.

LEVI: We walked into the Ironman Village. It's quiet but you can tell everyone is nervous and excited. Everyone's waiting for the race. There's thousands of people down there. I gave my dad a quick hug. I said, "I'm going to go get my bike. I'm going to get my stuff ready. You do the same."

TERRY: We started laying out our things for our transition.

LEVI: We laid out our special needs bags and our transition bags. Every athlete's bags are at this specific location according to your number, and they're all in a row. I took some neon tape, and walked over to our bags, put it on them so we could see them when we got out of the water, and we'd know which bags were ours.

Then we gathered up a couple friends who were doing the race and we prayed together and then it was time for us to go line up on the beach.

TERRY: I like to swim a little bit before an event. It helps me calm down, being in the water. We were in our wetsuits now. We went down to the lake and got in, just practicing. Levi didn't really need to do it, he just did it because I did. As we were in the water they played the National Anthem.

LEVI: People were lining up on the beach. There were 1,710 athletes registered but only 1,300 competing in the Ironman that day, due to the heat.

TERRY: Everybody went to their starting place. You place yourself in the line according to where you think you'll finish the swim.

LEVI: I was going to be ahead of my dad. I remember looking him in the eye in that moment and saying, "All right, Dad. Go get in line." I gave him a big hug. "Today, you're going to be an Ironman." I smiled at him. "I love you, and I'll see you out there."

Then I went and got in line. I looked back, but I couldn't see my dad anymore. The heat was ferocious. I could feel my feet, cooking on the sand.

The first Ironman had taught me important lessons. I focused on my goals. I was excited.

TERRY: I was beyond nervous. I was terrified. I stood on the beach trying to catch my breath. So many emotions. From shock to joy to panic to joy again. It overwhelmed me. And then the cannon went off.

LEVI: I was nervous for my dad. I knew he had never competed in an Ironman before. I thought back on our journey. I thought about how hard we trained and how much we talked about this moment. I thought about my dad experiencing the feeling of crossing the finish line, and me experiencing it again. That gave me tremendous energy.

Then the cannon went off. And I got in the water.

TERRY: My mind was focused on Levi when I heard the cannon boom. I knew he was way up in front of me. I had no idea when I'd see him again, because we wouldn't be together, Levi's so much faster than me.

When I heard that cannon blast, I knew: the race was on.

The line of competitors started moving forward. Even though I'm moving, I'm still 40-45 minutes from even getting in the water. I'm in line, ready to push my body to the limit, and feeling like at any moment I could bend over and throw up.

This is it. This is going to happen.

And now I'm trying to fight the memory of my Seattle-to-Portland ride. I'm trying to fight that, trying to move my legs, helpless as other swimmers zip by me, doing everything not to panic, trying to get the fear to subside.

That's when I realized: this Ironman thing is going to be much harder than I'd thought.

LEVI: *Alright, Levi,* I thought. *Here we go.* I'm fired up. I'm super-excited. I'm already visualizing the end of my swim in my mind.

I wasn't nervous. Not for myself. "This is my second Ironman," I kept repeating. "I am going to have a great swim and enjoy every minute of this race. This is going to be the best day ever."

I hit the water, thinking:

I can't wait for my dad to be an Ironman . . .

CHAPTER TEN

The Swim and the Bike

LEVI: As I was swimming, I remember thinking, "Okay, my dad's probably in the water now. I hope he's doing well." Because he had never done a race with this many people or an open water swim with so many athletes.

So I was a little nervous during the swim. It took me an hour and 24 minutes to do the swim, and the whole time, I'm thinking, "Alright, I wonder how my dad's doing. I hope he's doing okay." I'm praying, *Please, Lord, please be with my dad...*

TERRY: *You're doing awesome, Gurno,* I kept telling myself. But the truth is, I was struggling. Battling my mindset.

As I got closer and closer to entering the water, those feelings ramped up, and intensified. I remembered somebody had told me once that the best place to swim was close to the buoys, because most people try and swim away from them. So that was my strategy: swim as close to the buoys as possible.

My mind was a jumble of emotions. From fear, to excitement, back to fear, then to overwhelmed. Fear that I might panic. *You know how to swim, Gurno,* I reminded myself. *You've swum this distance before. So focus on that.*

I start swimming. I ended up stopping several times in the first half mile, to catch my breath. Treading water for a minute. You've got to be careful, Levi had warned me, because there are people coming behind you.

LEVI: If you stop swimming, the other competitors will be right on top of you—grabbing you, pushing you down, kicking and clawing to get past you.

TERRY: That just added to my anxiety.

I had to stop and calm my breathing down, and then keep going. And keep going. And going.

Man, that first loop—it was a struggle. The first two-thirds were a battle for my life. But in the last third, I found my rhythm. I'm moving through the water faster now. People are passing me on their second loop—you can tell when they pass, because they launch right by you fast, splashing and churning their arms and pushing you out of their way.

Fortunately, I got through that. I survived. I came out of the water and I thought, *I made my first loop. I just made my first loop!*

Then the second loop, I had a lot more confidence. I'd been swimming for awhile now. I was in a rhythm. I was kicking hard, head down between breaths, lengthening my body on each stroke, slipping my hands into the water almost silently. I felt like I was swimming downhill.

The rest of the swim was almost a breeze compared to the first loop. I took it one stroke at a time, breathing in, breathing out.

I was in the groove when I turned the last corner to head toward the shore. That's when I knew I was going to make it. *Okay, Gurno, you've got this.*

As I swam closer and closer, finally I got to a place where I could stand up, and walk out of the water. It was an hour and 51 minutes and a few seconds into my swim.

It was one of the most powerful moments of my life.

In my mind, my limiting belief was I could never swim that far. I was intimidated by open-water racing. Now, I was calm and determined.

I wore a big smile, as I headed toward the transition tent. It was time to get on the bike.

LEVI: I remember getting out of the swim and transitioning to my bike. I saw Sarah, my family, and my friends watching me. They're cheering me on through transition and screaming as I climb on my bike and started my first loop. "Go, Levi! Team Gurno!!" they yelled. It pumped me up! My sister, Chelsea, was the loudest. She is such an encouragement and gets so fired up for us every race. So of course, she was leading the charge for the "Team Gurno" support crew.

On the bike course, you go out around the northeast side of Lake Coeur d'Alene, 6.5 miles and then you turn back around, come back through town, then go 21.5 miles around the south end of the lake. Round trip mileage of each loop is 56 miles. I was feeling great out of the water and made it to Higgins Point, which was the first turnaround at mile 6.5, and I was heading back towards town.

As I'm pedaling, I'm thinking about one thing.

My dad.

Okay, I thought, *if my dad made it out of the water, then he's out on the bike course now, he's on his bike.* I was sure I'd see him, any minute.

I made it back to town. Approaching mile 13, there was a section where I was going to be turning left to head through town, and I suddenly started to worry, because I hadn't seen my dad yet. I knew this was the only opportunity, the only chance that I would have to see him, based upon where we were on our rides. I was about to head out on the long stretch of highway on the south side of the lake.

Please, let me see my dad! I remember praying, *I need to see my dad. I need to know he made it out. I need to know he's on his bike.* My fears were ramping up and my hopes were fading, and I was anxious and worried out of my head.

TERRY: I'm out of the water now. Quickly I raced into the tent, and grabbed my transition bag. I changed into my biking gear. I kept an eye on the time, noticing I'd spent 12 minutes in transition. When I raced back out, my family was standing outside the fence, watching me mount my bike. They're cheering for me, "Go, Dad, go! Go, Team Gurno!" and they're all pumped up and excited, and again I have the overwhelming sense, this overpowering feeling.

I cannot believe I'm doing this.

I cannot believe I'm in this race.

Then I'm on my bike. Time is ticking. I'm moving at a brisk clip. Suddenly it comes into my head: I wonder how Levi's doing. I wonder where Levi is.

I didn't know until afterwards, but Levi's wondering where *I* am. He's out on the bike course praying, "God, I need to know that my dad made it out."

LEVI: *Where's my dad?* I thought, as I rode. *Did something happen to him?*

TERRY: I knew Levi was out there somewhere. So I just started pedaling. I pedaled my heart out, with other competitors zooming past me, cheering loudly and encouraging me.

Suddenly there comes a place where I'm going to make a turn. *Steady as she goes, Gurno,* I remind myself, ripping around the corner. As I do, I see Levi's coming a block away, right toward me. It's the last place I thought might see Levi. I get to that corner, just about to make the turn, and Levi turns the other corner and he's coming towards me, yelling and whooping and screaming. He sees me and yells out, "Dad, you did it! you look *awesome,* you're doing great!"

LEVI: I came whipping around the corner, turned onto the next street, and there he was! And I just yelled, "Dad, Dad!" He gave me the thumbs up, and as we passed each other I shouted, "Nice job! Keep it up!"

TERRY: My emotions were going crazy. *Not a bad start,* I thought. *Maybe I can do this, after all.*

LEVI: At this point, I knew he'd made it out of the water. He was on his bike. I felt like I could relax a little. I could press on with my own race. I had a goal in mind and was keeping a solid pace. I knew my dad was capable of finishing the race on his own.

It's 8:15 in the morning now. I'm doing that first loop of the bike. The heat hadn't really hit its peak. It was about 90 degrees, which I had trained in. The heat slowly started creeping up on that first loop. As I made the turnaround at mile 34.5 and started heading back toward town, I was feeling good, energized, and mentally strong. Making sure I kept up on my nutrition and continued to pace myself.

I'd seen my dad heading out towards the south side of the lake as I was coming back towards town, and he was quite a ways behind me.

As we passed, I said to him, "Keep going, Dad. You can do it. Stay up on your water!"

He looked good, but it was hot, really hot! I knew he needed to keep a solid pace to finish the bike ride.

Now I was coming back through town. I had done a three-hour first loop of the bike. As I'm pedaling back through town, I see my family. They're cheering me on and I'm waving at them and I'm super-excited. I get to the portion of the bike where they had our special needs bags, which is mile 60. I had a bag with some electrolytes, some food and drinks to give me nutrition. After I refueled and stretched my legs for a minute, I got back on my bike and kept going.

It's at this point when I really began to feel the heat. It hit me like a wave! I had 52 miles to go, and another 3,445 miles of vertical feet to climb. I had to lock it in mentally and just keep going.

TERRY: That first loop on the bike, I felt great. I biked through downtown Couer d'Alene and got on the highway. You ride about 40 miles, round trip. The highway is the toughest part of the trip. You hit a hill and then it's a seven or eight percent grade for three miles.

Hills are not my strength. I can bike on the flat well enough, but the hills suck every ounce of strength out of me. I struggle, I lose speed, and slow down. But I stayed focused, and just kept pedaling, keeping a good pace.

Finally, I made my first loop. I come to downtown, my family's there, I look at my watch and I'm right where I thought I'd be. *Nice work, Gurno.* I pull up to the stop at mile 60, where there are more volunteers—they take your bike, give you your special needs bag. They have chairs in the shade, if you want to sit down.

I did. I sat down, and I ate. I drank from my nutrition bottle. That took about five minutes. Then got back on my bike and started riding again.

LEVI: It had been awhile since I'd seen my dad. Again, the worry started eating away at me.

TERRY: The challenge was not just that it was hot, but they had no cold water. So I couldn't drink anything cold. I recalled what Levi had warned me:

Fail to drink enough fluids on the bike, and you'll pay the price.

I was falling behind on my fluids. As I was pedaling, my thighs started to scream with pain. I ended up dropping my nutrition bottle by accident. *Gurno!* I screamed at myself. *There goes that!* I grimaced, hoping I'd pass somebody who could hand off another new bottle.

By the time looped back to town, I was fading fast. My energy level had significantly dropped. In horror, I noticed I was riding four miles an hour slower than I had been.

I knew I wasn't doing well, from a physical standpoint. However, I wasn't ready to give up. I stopped at the next aid station, just before I got back on the freeway. I poured water over my body, drank some Gatorade, then kept going as fast as I could, trying not to fall any further behind.

Reality set in. I was getting passed by other bikers, right and left. I knew Levi was having a phenomenal bike ride out there, somewhere, but I hadn't passed him in awhile. I started to worry something had happened.

Relax, I said to myself, gasping for breath as I started climbing uphill. I noticed I was going up this hill at three miles an hour, which is barely enough to stay upright. That's when I saw Levi again, coming right at me.

He yelled to me and said, "Dad, be really careful, it's dangerous out here!"

"I know!" I yelled back. And I kept going. Pedaling. Trying to shift gears. All the while struggling to overcome the hardest climb of the day.

With heavily-fatigued legs, I continued to pedal. *Keep riding, Gurno,* I told myself, *just keep riding.* But my legs screamed for rest.

I kept going. And going.

The blood in my head was pounding. My skin was burned, swollen and cracked from the sun. I rubbed the sweat from my eyes, feeling my fingers going numb on the handlebars. I felt like I was pedaling backwards. *Pedal, Gurno, pedal!* I was slowing down, but I was committed to fighting my body's need to surrender.

Time seemed to stop, then spin out endlessly. I could barely move my legs, and I knew I was facing a possible DNF.

Then the heat came.

CHAPTER ELEVEN

The Heat Is On

LEVI: By now, it had reached 107 degrees. It was 107 degrees in the air, but it was 145 degrees radiating off the pavement.

The intense heat was making everybody exhausted and demoralized. It was unlike anything I had ever seen or experienced.

I started getting worried for my dad. But I told myself, *Keep going*.

I was heading back out around the lake again, to finish my final loop. The heat was crazy, and I hadn't seen my dad. He had come through town, probably an hour and a half after me, and that was before the heat really started slamming us.

I was pedaling, getting concerned about his time, and his health. "Lord, be with him," I prayed.

Wiping the sweat from my eyes, I kept racing. About mile 80, as I'm pushing up this hill, I'm slumped down on the handlebars, lethargic. *Dude, you're losing it*. Mile 80 is what they call the make-it-or-break it point of the race. You're going up a three-mile, eight-percent grade hill. You realize you have 32 miles to go, plus a whole marathon to run, and by this time you're physically and mentally exhausted. I started slowing down, while still keeping a decent pace. It was at this time that I decided to throw my goal time of 13 hours out the window. My goal now was to beat my last year's time, and survive!

There's an aid station every 12 miles on the bike course. I had run out of all my water earlier, but I was positive there was an aid station coming up, so I thought, *I'll get more water and I'll be okay.*

Sure enough, as I'm going down this hill, I see an aid station on my left. At this point, I know I'm suffering from heat exhaustion because I can't think straight. I had passed this aid station before, but for whatever reason, in my confused mind I thought, "Oh wait, there's another one right around this corner for me on the right side, not the left."

And so I passed the aid station. I quickly realized that was going to be my only chance for water for another 12 miles, which is at least 40 minutes.

I ended up going 16 miles without water. My thirst was agonizing. I stopped sweating, which is a sign of dehydration. I started getting sleepy, and tired, literally wanting to fall asleep on my bike. My arm started going numb. I knew I had all the telltale signs of heat exhaustion, because I had taken an EMT course a few years prior to the race.

Needless to say, when I reached that next aid station, I was hurting. I quickly realized that every single aid station on the course was filled with dehydrated racers in the medical tent. Many were passed out. Others were hooked up to IVs. There were ambulances screaming up and down the street. I'd seen someone passed out on the side of the road, getting worked on by an EMT. It was insane!

When I reached the aid station, they looked at me and said, "Hey, you need to go to the medical tent." The race officials had said prior to the race that if a racer goes to the medical tent for heat exhaustion, they'd be pulled from the race. So I knew that if I went to the medical tent, they would disqualify me.

I said, "Listen, I know what I need to do." And what I did was: I packed my whole body with ice, everywhere that had main arteries. I packed my shirt, and my shorts, trying to cool down my internal body temp—my thighs, my core and my shirt and my helmet, everything. I packed everywhere I could with ice, then doused water all over my body.

I did that three times, to cool down my body temperature. Then I ate a Cliff Bar and drank a Gatorade, climbed back on my bike and kept going.

For the next three aid stations, that's what I did.

I would stop, pack my whole body with ice, and cool my body down.

I ended up stopping for a total of 45 minutes on the bike, just to cool myself down. Anything to keep from being hauled into the medical tent, and ending my race.

So now, as I'm headed back into town, I'm at mile 100 with 12 miles to go. I still had not seen my dad on the second loop. That told me he wasn't even at mile 80.

That's when the realization hit me.

Dad's not going to make the cut-off. He's not going to finish.

I didn't want to believe the words pulsing through my brain. It was the unthinkable. Our Ironman dream had been my source of strength. As I was riding, I started saying to myself, over and over, *He's not going to finish . . . He's not going to finish . . . He's not . . .*

At that moment, two friends of mine in a van pulled up alongside me. They asked me how I was doing, but all I could think about was my dad. "Hey, have you seen my dad?" I asked.

"Yeah," they said, pointing backwards on the course. "He's coming up the hill." It was the hill at mile 80, the three-mile brutal hill.

I was filled with hope just knowing that my dad was okay. Then the guys in the van hollered out, "Man, your dad's not looking good. He's not looking good at all."

I waved at my friends, refocused, and kept pedaling. I decided to believe Dad had the strength to drag himself up that hill, and make the cut-off time, even with the heat.

I bowed my head. Kept pedaling. And prayed. Hope was slipping away. At least I knew he was okay, and that he was still going. *Maybe,* I thought, in my groggy confusion, *he'll get a burst of energy. Maybe he'll finish the race . . .*

CHAPTER TWELVE

Disqualified

TERRY: I kept pedaling. Pedaling like crazy. Trying to generate enough power to complete my ride on time. Grinding away while the extreme heat of the sun beat down on me.

I reached the mile 80 checkpoint. Because I knew the course would have paramedics at every checkstop, and knowing the medics would pull me off the course if they saw any signs of dehydration or heat exhaustion, I felt relieved. I felt safe.

The checkstops would be my reality-check. That was my strategy.

As I approached mile 80, a race official and a paramedic sprinted up to me, in a panic.

"Listen," they said, "we think you need to get off your bike!"

I was confused. *Had they seen I was faltering? Was I showing some telltale sign of dehydration?*

"You need to get off your bike!" the medic repeated.

"Why do you think that?" I asked.

"Look," the medic said, his eyes staring into mine with a sense of clarity, "you don't look too good." He stopped talking, and his eyes went out to the race course. "You know you've got to make another ten miles. Ten miles, in an hour. And if you don't make it, you're going to be disqualified. Plus there's not as much support, once you get out there. You're really risking a lot if you leave."

I stared at him, in growing fear and confusion. "What are you telling me?" I asked. "Are you telling me my health is at risk? Is that what you're saying?" I kept sucking in breaths of hot air, trying to calm down. "Do you want me to quit because of my health? Is that what you're saying?"

"No, no, no," the medic insisted. "I'm not telling you that. I'm just recommending that if you don't feel like you can make ten miles in an hour, I suggest you get off. *Now.*"

I looked at the two guys and shook my head. "I'm not getting off." And off I pedaled. As fast as I could.

I kept going.

LEVI: I remember coming down that hill, as he's coming up. And I see him. *Dad!* It was right as I was approaching the hill, and I see my dad, so I put on my brakes, and at this point I'm just yelling and screaming at him. "Dad, you have to be *careful!* Don't hurt yourself! Keep up on your nutrition! Keep drinking water! Cool yourself down! This is *dangerous!*" Because he looked so exhausted. He looked in a state of confusion.

My dad had a friend of his riding next to him—a friend who wasn't actually in the race. The race officials had let his friend ride on the side of the road, to make sure people like my dad were okay. He was riding alongside my dad and encouraging him.

I passed by my dad. I glided downhill, then looked back over my shoulder. I thought about turning around and riding with my dad, even though I knew it would mean both of us wouldn't finish, we'd both be disqualified. But my dad saw me, waved, and yelled back: "Keep it up, Bud! You can do it! I'm being careful!"

It was at that moment—mile 102, with 10 miles to go—when I knew he wasn't going to finish.

TERRY: My feet were slipping out of the pedals. My bones ached. *It's all for nothing,* I thought, *if I don't finish. It all means nothing, if I quit now.*

Other cyclists screamed past. I dropped my head, and kept going.

Up ahead, there was another hill. A brutal, three-mile climb. I pedaled, and climbed, even though I was getting dizzy and baking with fever.

I kept pedaling. And climbing. And climbing. Almost tipping over, from going so slow. I resolved to pedal straight to the finish or until my body gave out altogether, whichever came first.

Finally, I reached the flat part of the hill, the plateau. Instantly, I started feeling better. I was nearing the mile 90 turnaround, which was a cut-off point. If I hadn't reached that point by a certain time, I knew it was the end. I'd be DNF'd.

I rode flat-out, across the plateau, the hillside streaming past. I felt deep relief, believing that I might make the cut-off. I had a chance. I kept riding, and riding . . .

As I looked up the road, standing in the middle I saw a guy. Waving his arms.

At first, I thought he was waving me on, urging me to go faster. I lurched ahead. He stepped more into my path. I heard him shouting. I couldn't make it out. I straddled the bike, my fists locked around the handlebars, my legs churning but wavering, trying to crush this course with my every effort. In my tired mind, I heard the guy repeating himself:

"You didn't make it!"

What?

"You didn't make it! You missed the 90-mile cut-off! Your race is over!"

My race is over? I recoiled, gasping. *Maybe he doesn't understand,* I thought, *that I'm not dehydrated.* As the bike carried me up to the guy, who was still waving his arms, our eyes locked. I'm sure I was trembling, in expectation of the words he was going to say.

"Your race is over," he repeated "You have to get off. You're disqualified."

CHAPTER THIRTEEN

Bent, but Unbroken

TERRY: *Disqualified.* I could feel the bike shaking underneath me. *I'm disqualified. Done.* It didn't make sense.

I thought of everything I'd sacrificed for this moment. Everything Levi had sacrificed. The sacrifices our family had made. In all our plans, there was never any way I wasn't going to finish. This wasn't in our game plan.

Can I please keep riding? I wanted to plead with the race official. I wanted somebody to tell him this was so much more than a race to me.

I took a deep breath. *My race is over.* Everything Levi and I had talked about wasn't going to happen. We wouldn't be Ironmen together.

What would Levi say, when he learned?

LEVI: The heat was still blasting down, as I crossed the finish line for the bike race. All around me, I could see other cyclists, crumpled over and staggering.

As I hurried to the transition area, I thought of my dad. I changed into my running shorts. I felt fresh, my legs springy. As soon as I raced out of the changing tent, my whole family was there, waiting for me.

I received a joyous hug from my mom. As we're embracing, I said, "Hey, I just want you to know, I don't think Dad's going to finish. So just prepare yourself."

It's funny. Even though I was telling her to prepare herself, I wasn't mentally prepared myself for dad not finishing. I knew the reality of where my dad was. I felt pride in knowing we'd both given this race absolutely everything we had. Not to mention that I was ahead of my previous Ironman time. Everything would work out.

So with the cheers of my family to fortify me, I started my run.

TERRY: It's weird. Even though I'd been disqualified, I was so happy.

Happy I'd been in the race. Happy I'd given it all I could on that day. Happy I'd summoned the passion to pursue my dream.

It just wasn't enough to finish.

LEVI: I'm running now. On the side of the road, volunteers are spraying me with water and offering me ice. I'm running and meanwhile my mind's flashing to thoughts of my dad.

I make it to the first turnaround, out around the lake, which is mile 6.5. Afterward, you head back into town, for your first loop. As I'm running, my friend Luke rides up on his bike, coming alongside me.

"Hey, dude," I asked, "how's my dad?"

Luke's voice was low. He looked bummed. "Dude," he said, "your dad didn't make it. He got cut off at the mile 90 mark."

I stared off down the race course. "Is he okay?" I asked.

"I think so, man, but I'm not sure."

Luke then told me he'd seen my dad with the medical staff. So now, I'm freaking out. *Did he crash?* I wonder. I tell Luke, "I need you to call my mom, and see what's going on."

Instantly, Luke got my mom on the phone. "Tell him his dad is fine," she said, "but he didn't make the cut. He's heading back into town right now."

TERRY: I got a ride back into town, along with the others who were disqualified. We came back to town on the bus. I felt my anxiety swell as I strolled into the transition area, unsnapped my helmet, combed my fingers through my sweaty hair, and changed out of my cycling gear.

That's when I saw Nancy, by the medical entrance. She had heard I'd been sent back to town.

Sensing my dejection, Nancy gave me a hug, and kissed my cheek. She held me at arm's length to survey the damage, then gave me an even bigger hug. Nancy told me that Levi was about to be at the halfway point of the marathon and he wanted to see me.

Wow, I thought. *Levi's done really well.* I was proud of him. I smiled and looked down at my aching, swollen knees. I was hurt, emotionally spent, and physically drained. My biggest regret wasn't the throbbing pain all over my body—it was not seeing the dream of completing the Ironman to the finish line with my son.

LEVI: Even though I was worried about my dad, I was reluctant to alter my running pace. I tried to focus on the journey ahead.

As I ran, I happened to bump into another competitor, named

Don. For awhile, Don and I ran together, neck and neck, at the same pace. We started talking. It's good to have someone to talk to, when you're at that part of the race—by now, it was 108 degrees. "Let's run together," I suggested, feeling the heat waves surging up from the pavement, "so we can keep our minds off how much this hurts."

I could get my mind off my feet. And the heat. But I couldn't get my thoughts away from my dad.

TERRY: I didn't feel bad for myself. Not at all. It wasn't my day, but at least I was in the race.

But my daughters—Chelsea and Ali—they were crying. My sister was crying. My wife Nancy was crying. They were devastated for me.

As we were all headed back to the race course, Levi came running in, on his way through downtown. Seeing us, he sped up. I found myself wondering what he would say, as he came running up to me.

As soon as he saw me, I could tell Levi became choked up. He fell into my arms. He sobbed and said, "Dad, I'm sorry, I'm sorry, I'm so sorry, Dad!" Just over and over. Sobbing from deep down inside, as he held me.

Wiping the tears from my eyes, I wrapped Levi up in my arms. It was an exhausting, exhilarating moment as father and son. A moment no one could ever take from us. My brother-in-law, through his own tears, thought to snap a photograph.

It's the photo on the cover of this book.

LEVI: At this point, my spirits were crushed. I almost broke down, because I was so disheartened.

I had told Luke to tell my mom I really wanted to see Dad, when I came back into town, and to please make sure he's there. So when

I got into town, and was approaching my family, I was in this weird fog, because of the heat. But then I saw my dad. I really didn't know if I could hold in my emotions. All I remember is losing it, and giving him a big hug.

"I'm sorry, Dad, I'm so sorry!" That's all I could think to say. Tears gushed out. Gripping tight to his shoulders, I held on for dear life, not wanting to let go.

My dad just looked at me. "Listen, Bud," he said. "I'm not sorry. And you don't need to be sorry. I gave it my all. I gave it everything I could, and you know what?" My heart began to beat faster, waiting to hear what he'd say. "Today, my race didn't go as planned. And my race may be done today. But I'm not finished."

"I'm going to finish an Ironman," he continued, staring me straight in the eye. "We're going to finish. Together."

He took a deep breath, then let it out, like these were the most important words he'd ever said. "But listen," he continued, pointing me back toward the course, "your race isn't over. You still have a race to finish. And we're going to be here, cheering you on. So go, Bud. Go finish your race."

TERRY: When I said those words, hugging Levi, I felt like a 500-pound weight had been removed from my shoulders.

Did you seriously just say that, Gurno? I thought. All the intense emotions of being disqualified from the race came rushing back. *Yes,* I said to myself, with firm commitment. *Yes, I did.*

It wasn't the moment Levi and I had hoped for. It wasn't the triumphant moment we'd trained for. But it was a moment I wouldn't trade for anything. All our emotions, as father and son, came pouring out, in that moment, as our family stood there. It was a moment for all of us. Tears mixed with sweat stung my eyes as I watched Levi turn and jog off, to continue his marathon.

LEVI: "I'm going to be here, waiting for you," my dad said.

So I went back on the course. I kept running. I had 13.1 miles left to run. Now I had a new goal in mind.

I was going to finish this thing. For the both of us.

TERRY: Levi is such an encourager. I just knew that if he couldn't encourage me the rest of the way, he'd find somebody else to encourage.

LEVI: My first Ironman, I finished at 14 hours and 9 minutes. I wanted to break 13 hours on this one, but the intense heat threw that goal out of my mind. "You know what?" I told myself, "I just want to finish, for my dad, and be safe."

Two miles left. My legs were numb. To get my mind off the heat and my legs, I started thinking about how I was going to propose to Sarah. I switched from running to a run/walk combo. I'd run to the next turn. To the next tree. Then walk for a minute.

Coming to the last leg of the race, I could feel my whole lower body go numb. I could barely feel anything. I caught up with Don, and we were running and digging deep for the final push.

Now we're coming into town. Running hard. Approaching Sherman Avenue, the finish line, the end of the race.

Don turned onto Sherman with me. Suddenly there were thousands of people, cheering us on—friends and family, total strangers, all clapping and yelling and screaming for us. Running down the Ironman chute to the finish line, you don't really want to run it with anybody. It's *your* moment. I ended up telling Don, "Hey, bro, go ahead. You go first. This is your moment." It was his first Ironman.

"No, man," Don pleaded, "you go first."

"No way, dude," I laughed, "your wife is right there. Go, finish, run!" And so Don ran ahead, and finished. I crossed the finish line right behind.

Immediately I saw Sarah and my whole family, right there. My mom, my dad, my friends, everybody. I threw my hands in the air in triumph.

Wow! 140.6 miles! 108-degree heat! I just finished another Ironman!

TERRY: Watching Levi cross the finish line, I was flooded with different emotions. A lump in my throat, tears in my eyes. Seeing Levi finish his race and our whole family embracing him erased the throbbing pain in my knees.

LEVI: The cool thing is, when I finished, someone in my family hurried over and said, "Hey, do you know what time you got?" At this point, I wasn't even thinking about it. Certainly I was behind my previous year's time.

"No," I said, "what time did I get?"

They replied, "14 hours and 8 minutes."

Oh my gosh! Seriously? Yes!

TERRY: Levi had literally beat his last year's time by *one minute!*

LEVI: After embracing Sarah and giving her a big hug and kiss, accepting hugs from my entire family, and the crowd cleared away, I remember going up to my dad. He was telling me how proud he was of me. I could see he was in immense pain but brimming with energy.

"Dad," I said, my voice cracking with emotion as I hugged him, "again, I'm so sorry!"

Dad met my heartache with a smile. "Hey, don't worry about it," he said. Then he released me from his embrace, and all the noise around us faded to nothing. "I'm going to be an Ironman," he repeated.

I swallowed hard. Speechless. One look in his eyes told me he was serious. Dead serious.

TERRY: They placed Levi's Ironman finisher's medal around his neck. I felt the tears well up in my eyes. We all snapped pictures.

"Let's get a picture with you wearing it," Levi urged me.

"I'm not going to do that," I said.

Levi looked at me, astonished. "Why not?"

"I didn't earn it," I told him. "So I'm not going to wear it."

And I didn't. I didn't put the Ironman medal on. Nor did I buy any Ironman finisher's stuff, because I didn't finish.

But you know what? I wasn't resentful. I wasn't bummed. I wasn't sad. I was nothing but determined. *I will FINISH an Ironman.*

Did I expect that I'd feel this good? No way. But my mind was already focused on what lay ahead. First up, I had to tell my whole family what I'd already committed to.

I wasn't just going to compete in the next Ironman. I was going to *finish* the next Ironman.

My race was only beginning.

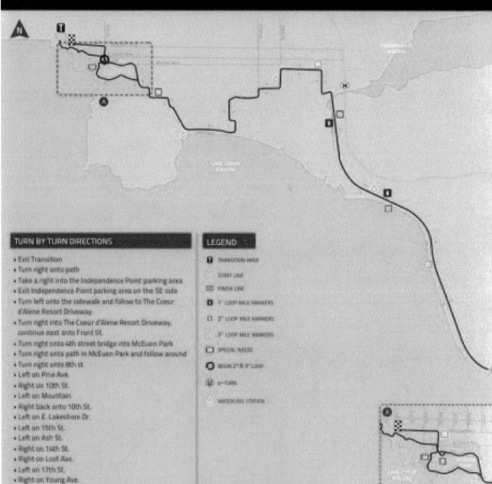

TURN BY TURN DIRECTIONS

- Exit Transition
- Turn right onto path
- Take a right into the Independence Point parking area
- Exit Independence Point parking area on the SE side
- Turn left onto the sidewalk and follow to The Coeur d'Alene Resort Driveway
- Turn right into The Coeur d'Alene Resort Driveway, continue east onto Front St.
- Turn right onto 4th street bridge into McEuen Park
- Turn right onto path in McEuen Park and follow around
- Turn right onto 8th st
- Left on Pine Ave.
- Right on 10th St.
- Left on Mountain
- Right back onto 10th St.
- Left on E. Lakeshore Dr.
- Left on 15th St.
- Left on Ash St.
- Right on 14th St.
- Right on Lost Ave.
- Left on 17th St.
- Right on Young Ave.
- Left on 19th St.
- Right on Mullan Ave.
- Right on 23rd St.
- Left on Ashton Rd.
- Right on Centennial Trail (parallels CDA Lake Dr.)
- Turn Around past Aid Station 3 near Silver Beach Marina
- Start second and third loop
- Turn right onto 4th street and across the bridge
- Continue north on 4th street
- Turn left onto Sherman avenue to the Finish Line

LEGEND

- TRANSITION AREA
- START LINE
- FINISH LINE
- 1ˢᵗ LOOP MILE MARKERS
- 2ⁿᵈ LOOP MILE MARKERS
- 3ʳᵈ LOOP MILE MARKERS
- SPECIAL NEEDS
- BEGIN 2ⁿᵈ & 3ʳᵈ LOOP
- U-TURN
- WATER/AID STATION

Start Elevation: 2,137 ft • Finishing Elevation: 2,140 ft • Gain: 723 ft

PART THREE

MR. UNFINISHED BUSINESS

CHAPTER FOURTEEN

Drawing a Line in the Sand

TERRY: I'd approached the first Ironman with fear. *Could I make the swim? Could my knees hold up, after biking 112 miles? After running a marathon?*

The second year, I awakened something inside myself. I realized: *I can do this.*

LEVI: We had a year to prepare. But zero room for error in our preparation. This was going to be the year my dad crossed the finish line, and I was all in with him again.

We knew the task would be too daunting, too overwhelming, if we didn't make changes. Changes in our training. Our diet. Our equipment. Our race-day nutrition.

TERRY: One thing I realized: I didn't eat enough, I didn't drink enough, during my first Ironman. I wasn't eating the right thing, or the right amount of calories per hour. And the need to have salt with me was critical. I decided I'd start drinking five Gatorades a day, five days before the event. The reason I'd lost four miles an hour during the first race, and couldn't get it back, was my nutrition.

Ironically, I didn't tell my wife right away that I was doing another Ironman. I knew Nancy wouldn't be happy. I remembered our conversation, when I'd told her I was competing in the first Ironman.

She made me promise: "*One time,* Terry. Right? You're going to try this once, and that's it?"

"Yes," I'd assured her.

After I'd recommitted my heart to competing in the second Ironman, I knew I'd have to tell Nancy. It took a moment before she realized what I'd just said. She looked at me. Instantly, I knew I didn't need to worry.

"We're going to get you a new bike," she said. She started listing all the things we were going to do, next year. "We're going to make sure you have the right equipment. We have to do this right," she insisted, with a look in her eyes that said she wanted me to finish this time.

LEVI: Mom looked at him, and said, "Okay, we're going to need a better bike. And we're going to get you a coach, and you're going to finish next year." They both recommitted, right then and there.

(Oh, and remember the big plans I had for the day after Ironman? Well, Sarah said *yes!*)

It was a couple of days later when my dad's vow to embark on another Ironman finally hit me. "Oh, whoa. You're literally going to do it *again*, next year?" Just hearing those words from my dad lifted a weight from my shoulders. "Okay," I said, "if you're doing it, our plan is to do it *together*. I'm going to do it with you."

"Are you sure? Bud, this is your third one!"

"Yes, Dad," I said. It didn't just feel good to say that. It felt *amazing*. "I'm doing it with you."

TERRY: "Whoa, Terry's doing it *again* next year?"

Hearing our friends and family say those words energized me. It lifted the burden I felt I'd placed on my family. They were so disappointed, the day I'd been disqualified. Disappointed for *me*. They knew how badly I wanted it, and didn't get it.

That whole year, between the first and second Ironman, I received a ton of support from my family. They were sacrificing a lot for me. Sacrificing time. Sacrificing finances. Re-adjusting their schedules. Encouraging me, with positive talk, about how it would feel when I crossed the finish line. When I looked at them, all I heard in my mind was *We're doing this together. As a family.*

LEVI: We began training together for the next Ironman in February of the following year. But we started workouts sooner than that.

We looked into getting him a new bike.

TERRY: Actually, what happened was *Levi* got a new bike, and I took the bike Levi had used for his Ironman. So technically, we both had new bikes.

LEVI: We started working out through the summer after Ironman. You need to give your body time to recover, after an Ironman. We started hitting it hard a month later. Getting back into the mindset. Getting our spirit fully engaged. Getting in shape, getting focused.

TERRY: For the first time in decades, I was working out almost daily. Running. Walking. Biking. Swimming.

It wasn't until we signed up for the half Ironman, which was coming in June, that I realized something was wrong with Levi...

CHAPTER FIFTEEN

The Half Ironman

LEVI: In February and March, we started training together. Bike training. Swim training. We did a couple of 75-mile bike rides. In May, we started pushing the pace. We had one long 100-mile training ride, and I remember this ride because that's when I realized there was something going on with my body.

40 miles into that ride, my entire lower body started cramping up. My legs seized up on me. I squeezed my eyes tight, and tried to concentrate on the ride, but all I could feel was this immense, throbbing pain.

My mind worked furiously to understand what was happening. In all my rides, I'd never experienced this before. I had kept up on my nutrition, stayed hydrated, stretched...I did all the right things. My body felt like it was giving up on me. *Maybe I've just been over-training,* I thought—we hadn't taken much time off, from training.

I ended up pushing through the ride. I rode the last 60 miles completely cramped up, knifelike jabs screaming up my legs.

It was after that ride when I realized, "Okay, there's something going on." Suddenly, training was a lot harder. I began cramping at anything over 40 miles on the bike. I cramped up on anything over 5 miles on the run.

I was getting migraine headaches. Feeling lethargic. Extremely tired. My body was reaching its breaking point.

We kept training though. Five days a week. It was a month and a half before the half Ironman.

I tried pushing through the pain. Easier said than done. Finally, I saw a doctor, and got my blood work done. Everything was fine. "You're tired," the doctor told me. "Your body is fatigued. You need to rest."

But we kept on training together. The half Ironman was a defining moment in our prep for the full Ironman. The night before, I felt a wave of emotions—fear, dread—wondering how much punishment my body could take.

TERRY: They had moved the full Ironman to August, and scheduled a half Ironman—a 70.3 race—for late June.

"Hey," we'd decided, "let's do that. It'll give us a good indication of how well we're doing. How well our training is coming. If we're ahead, if we're right on pace or if we're going to be in trouble."

I was excited to do the half Ironman. *This is the perfect test. It's like a stepping-stone, to doing the full Ironman. This is going to show me where I'm at,* I thought. *Bring it on!*

LEVI: The race started. During the swim, I felt no problems. But I started cramping up severely, during the bike. And the entire run, I was experiencing the worst cramps I'd ever had. A couple of times, the cramps dropped me to the ground. I was lying on the hard concrete trying to get the cramps out of my leg. I ended up finishing the half Ironman, but it wasn't pretty.

My dad ended up finishing in eight hours and 18 minutes. An hour longer than he'd planned.

TERRY: *Eight hours and 18 minutes!?!?*

It couldn't be! What it showed me was I was not on pace to finish a full Ironman. I finished with just twelve minutes to spare. Not only that, but I was in a lot of pain. My back was screaming on the run. My knees almost buckled as I crossed the finish line.

I was incredibly discouraged. I knew I was not on pace to finish the full Ironman. My mind was consumed with one thought: *You're done.* At that moment, I really didn't care.

You asked for it, Gurno, I heard replaying in my mind. *This race showed you who you really are.*

LEVI: We realized he wasn't on-pace to finish the full Ironman in enough time. And for me, there was something going on with my body, something bad.

We had ten weeks, until the full Ironman.

TERRY: I was losing hope. I was now officially at the breaking point. We'd been grinding it out for nearly a year, in preparation for Ironman.

In our dedication to achieve the impossible, in our commitment to training daily, in our exhaustion, we'd underestimated the enormity of the challenge, and overlooked one crucial thing we'd need to push us over the top.

We needed a *coach.* As I showered, and rinsed the sweat and pain from the half Ironman off my body that night, I resolved to find somebody.

Fast.

CHAPTER SIXTEEN

Enter Coach Corey

LEVI: Ten weeks before the starting gun of the Coeur d'Alene Ironman, Coach Corey came into the picture.

TERRY: Corey McKenna's a familiar face in the Ironman community. Corey'd competed in Ironman World Championships, with twelve full Ironman finishes, including Coeur d'Alene four times.

I told Corey about my Ironman, the year before, and the half Ironman I'd just completed.

"I'm not on pace to finish," I confessed. "I need help."

Corey listened. Immediately he gave me a plan. We started doing specific workouts, based on how I'd performed in the last year's Ironman, and the half Ironman.

LEVI: That was when a lot of things switched for my dad, physically. Coach Corey pushed him, further and further. He created workouts my dad didn't have before. Soon, my dad started dialing it in, doing really well.

TERRY: I was haunted by not finishing last year. That drove me.

What drove me even more was Corey's assessment that I was far from ready. *Great, just what I needed to hear.* I kept having to fight that mindset that I'm not ready, I'm not prepared, I'm not going to be able to do this.

It was an ongoing battle. One of the things I did mentally was to recognize those voices or thoughts as soon they happened, and immediately shut them down. That allowed me to move forward, and not be so panicked.

Training with Corey revitalized me. He rode with me. He took videos of me while I was riding. He pointed out things I was doing to lose power.

He ran with me, and shot videos of me running, which showed me where I wasn't running efficiently.

The same with swimming. He'd paddleboard next to me, and point out things that would help somebody like me, an average guy who is just trying to finish under the 17-hour mark.

Every week, he gave me a training schedule, based on how I'd performed the week before. Then he educated me on nutrition.

The year before, I had been eating Cliff Bars. Cliff Bars give you a lot of fuel, calories and carbohydrates, but I'd discovered they were hard for me to swallow when I was riding. Corey pointed me to Power Bars, which are chewier.

"When you're riding," he told me, "anytime you're taking in food, drink water. And when you're not taking food, drink your hydration drink. Because if you're eating and drinking your hydration drink at the same time, it can really affect your stomach, and make your sick."

Corey also told me to eat every 15 minutes on the bike. "Whether you feel like it or not," he insisted.

My hydration drink became Blue Gatorade. Gatorade's the drink they have available on the Ironman course. I didn't want to switch drinks while I was out there. I wanted the same stuff going in me that I trained with. I also never changed my equipment—whether it's socks, shoes, shorts, anything—from my race day gear.

"You don't want to change anything," Corey emphasized, "come race day."

Corey's coaching was the prize I'd been questing after. I was getting stronger. I was getting faster. I was excited by the challenge of hitting the starting line with Corey's training regimen under my belt. I knew that if Corey thought I could conquer the Ironman, then it could be done.

I'd assumed, with all my training, that Levi would be hitting his training stride, too.

I shouldn't have assumed anything. Looking back, it's unbelievable that I didn't see what was happening. A week before the race, Levi pulled me aside.

And Levi dropped the bomb.

Above left: Terry, age 3.
Above right: Terry, age 13.

1973 Talbot Hill Tigers. Terry in back row, #76. Three years before, Terry's dad left him at this same park to walk home alone.

Terry (seated, right) with his brothers and sisters at the Morningside house, 1966.

"Mr. Personality."
Levi, age 3.

Right top: Levi, 8th grade. Bottom right: Levi, age 13, and Terry at New York City.
Left: Senior night, Coeur d'Alene High School, 2003.

Levi's story. Bottom left: with wife Sarah, after the 2015 Ironman.
Bottom right: Levi hugs Nancy, after completing his first Ironman, 2014.

Levi reaches the finish line at Coeur d'Alene, 2014.

Ironman 2015.
The emotional reunion
between father and son,
after Terry's
disqualification.

Bottom left: Family
cheering Levi, Ironman
2015.
Bottom right: Levi's
second Ironman finish.

Ironman 2016. Top left: Terry finishes the swim. Top right: Terry on the bike. Bottom right: Terry, in immense pain, on the run. Bottom left: Terry's family cheers him on.

Ironman 2016. Finished business: an exhausted Terry reaches the finish line, into the arms of Levi.

Father and son, collaborating on the *unFinished Business* manuscript, Coeur d'Alene, May 2018.

CHAPTER SEVENTEEN

Levi's Decision

LEVI: I had pushed my body full-throttle for months. For months, I'd tried to ignore the pain. The cramps were so violent, it felt like I was being stabbed.

The month before the race, I started to pull back on my training. My plan now was to do the whole Ironman with my dad, but at a slower pace. "Hey, I don't really need to go out and kill myself," I reasoned. "I'm just going to hang with my dad the entire Ironman and make sure he gets to the finish line."

That was my thought process.

Three weeks before the race, however, I started sleeping through my alarm in the morning—which is not like me. The migraines had been getting worse. It felt like my brain was going to explode. *Slow down,* the doctor had warned me. Although I'd raced and completed two triathlons, my body was responding with less and less enthusiasm to racing a third.

TERRY: Basically, Levi's body was saying *I need a break*. Every time we'd ride together, he'd start cramping. Same thing with running. He'd cramp to the point where he just couldn't go on.

LEVI: I was torn. I wanted to do this, for my dad. I wanted to finish what we had started.

TERRY: So I started asking him, "Levi, are you sure you should do this?"

"I'm doing this," Levi insisted, through his pain.

LEVI: My dad had told me on and off, "Bud, I don't know if you can do it." I convinced him everything was okay. "No, Dad. This is our plan and I'm doing it with you, just like I told you I would."

TERRY: He was committed. Committed to doing it for me. Doing it *with* me. He wouldn't have done it himself—more than anything, he wanted to be there for me and with me, and finish the goal we'd started.

He tried keeping it to himself, hiding his appearance with that same Levi smile. I was concerned with what he was doing to his body.

LEVI: I thought about it for a few days. Letting the reality of it sink in. I realized that continuing to train was doing more damage than anything. I wanted to follow through on my commitment. I wanted to see my dad's dream all the way to the finish line.

But I had a nagging feeling I couldn't shake. It was a week before the race when I went over to my parents' house.

"First off," I told my dad, "I want to apologize."

"Apologize?" my dad replied, giving me a blank look. "For what?"

"I'm not going to be able to do the race," I said. "My body is just not where it needs to be. My body can't take it." Then I said the three words I thought would shatter my dad's dream. "Dad, I'm out."

TERRY: "Dad, I just can't do it," Levi said.

LEVI: I stared at my dad's face. Waiting to see his reaction.

To my surprise, he seemed *relieved.*

TERRY: I actually *was* relieved. I felt better. More than anything, I was concerned for Levi's health—I didn't realize how much until he told me that day, "I'm not going to do it." When he said that, I felt one of the most profound realizations on the whole journey.

Okay. This is good, I thought. Levi's decision got me focused. Part of my focus had been worrying about him. But when he said that, I was like, *Okay. Now I know.*

I got this.

LEVI: Ultimately, I think it helped him focus more, because he didn't have to worry about me.

It was at that moment when I said, "Dad, I can't do the race with you, but I'm going to be there for you, just like you've been there for me in the past. I'm going to be there, every step of the way. I'm going to coach you up, and we're going to make sure you get to the finish line."

TERRY: He urged me, "This is it, Dad. This is what we talked about. This is *your* story."

Those words roused me. They uplifted me. In that moment, my mission came into sharper focus. I realized I hadn't been completely focused on my race. Because the minute Levi told me, I felt an unexplainable sense of relief. Now, I was intensely focused on what I had to do.

CHAPTER EIGHTEEN

The Bike Wreck

TERRY: As I fixed my mind on my last-minute prep for the race, an oppressive weight settled on me. My thoughts flew back to an event that nearly ended my race before it even started.

A month before the race, I wrecked my bike.

It was a beautiful Saturday afternoon. I'd decided to do a ride around Hayden Lake, which is a 32-mile ride from my home. Hayden Lake is perfect for Ironman prep, as there are lots of hills climbing up and down, to give you a good workout.

On the back side of Hayden Lake, you come to a steep hill. Usually, I pedal *up* the hill, and it's brutal. On this particular day, I was riding downhill.

Now, I have a bad tendency to brake a little too much, when going downhill. It's a bad habit I'd picked up, and one I was determined to fix. *You've got a race coming up, Gurno,* I thought. *There's no time to be timid. Time to start pushing it.*

So down I glide, at a fast clip. I'm riding downhill, alongside a friend of mine. We're really flying down this hill, when suddenly, up ahead, there's this turn. *Let off the brakes,* I'm telling myself.

So I'm not braking.

That's when I realize: *I'm taking this hill too fast! Slow down!* Because of my speed, I can't make the insanely-tight turn that's coming up. So what do I do? I aim my bike toward the road shoulder. Unfortunately, there's gravel there. *Hit the brakes, Gurno.* As soon as I do, the brakes lock up, and I fishtail, going downhill at 30 miles an hour.

What did you expect, Gurno? Let up!

In a panic, I release my brake. Straighten the bike out. Too late! I go careening off the road, and flying off the shoulder.

Below me, I see a drop-off. It's not straight down, but it's a 40-feet drop and the angle is significant enough to cause my eyes to widen in fright.

I fly off the shoulder, my shoes strapped into the pedals. I'm clipped into my pedals and my bike is stuck to my feet. The ground below is rushing toward me. *This is it.*

Boom! I slam to the ground—fortunately for me, into this thick underbrush. I roll through it. At some point, my bike disengages from my feet, and I roll into another thick bush and that ultimately stops me.

I lay there, groaning, catching my breath. I look around. Instantly I see it's a miracle I didn't hit a tree. There are a *lot* of trees. A low branch or a sharp bough sticking out of the ground, and I'd be dead. But I'm okay. I can move. Nothing seems broken.

Up above, I hear my friend shouting my name. I can tell by the look of shock on his face he's seen the whole thing. He's yelling for me and I yell back, "I'm okay!"

I crawl back up the hillside, on my hands and knees. My friend's already rescued my bike from the crash. He checks me out, looking me all over, incredulous. I have a big welt and puncture wound on my shin and it's pretty scraped up. Blood is seeping out. When I first look at it, I'm sure it's a compound fracture. Fortunately, I can't feel any pain—I can't feel anything at all.

There happened to be a car following us up the hill. When they passed one bike rider, but not two, they turned around and came back. The driver—a woman who worked at the local hospital—realized I was in shock. I stood there, dazed, unable to speak. She got out a blanket, and placed it around me. My friend called his wife, who came and drove us to the Urgent Care, where they took X-rays of my leg.

"Nothing is broken," the tech told me, shaking his head. "Just a bad bruise, and you do have a cut with a little bit of gravel inside. Other than that, you're okay."

Okay? Man, was I relieved! I thought my Ironman race was over.

The next day, I didn't hurt anywhere. *Impossible,* I thought.

Even more impossible, I never lost a day of training.

Luckily, my bike had survived the crash. It took a beating, but it was still in one piece.

That crash off the hillside is what I was thinking of, my last day of prep before the Ironman race. I'd taken my bike in, for a pre-race tune-up. They cleaned it, and gave me new tires.

Later that day, the phone rang.

"Hey, we've got some bad news for you." It was the guy from the bike shop.

My mind froze. *Now what?*

"The frame of your bike is cracked," he said.

"You're kidding!"

"No, sir. It's cracked, all right."

"What does that mean?"

"Well," he explained, with a deep sigh. "We don't recommend you ride it, because it could fall apart. I wouldn't ride it," he said. "But the call is yours."

As I hung up, I considered this news. *What were my options?* None. I *had* no other options. My options were to ride the bike, or get a new bike. Coach Corey's mantra had been *Nothing new, no changes before the race.* So that option was out.

Later, I picked up the bike from the shop. I inspected it closely. Trying to find the crack in the frame. I couldn't find anything.

I sure hope this thing doesn't collapse on me, I sighed, thinking about the 112-mile ride ahead of me. *Otherwise, my goal of conquering Ironman will remain nothing but a dream.*

CHAPTER NINETEEN

"Mr. Unfinished Business"

TERRY: The phone kept ringing and ringing off the hook. Friends calling. Family calling. "Are you *really* going through with this, Terry? Are you gonna make it, this year?" That was *the question*. I told myself to focus on the race. *Stay calm. No pressure.* Everywhere I went, it seemed like people were always asking *the question* and the phone was always ringing and ringing.

One day, right before Ironman, Levi and I were heading to Seattle for a speaking engagement. As we're packing, my phone rings. A number I don't recognize.

"Hello?"

"Hey Terry," says a voice on the other end, "this is Ryan Collingwood, of the Coeur d'Alene Press. We heard your story, about falling short of finishing the Ironman last year, that you and your son are going to try to do it again. We'd like to do an article about you guys."

"You're kidding me," I said. *Great,* I'm thinking, *just as I'm trying to get out of town.*

LEVI: It was a few days after I'd told my dad I wasn't going to do the race that the newspaper reached out. "Hey, we want to interview you guys, we want to hear your story."

TERRY: I was preoccupied with the upcoming Ironman race as well as trying to get out of town, but we decided to meet the reporter, Ryan Collingwood, on our way.

Collingwood met us at the local park. He interviewed us. Snapped a couple of pictures. That was that. I'm ready to get in our car, go to Seattle.

As we're wrapping up, Levi tells Collingwood, "Here's a picture my uncle took. You might find this interesting." Levi gave him the photo of he and I hugging after I'd been disqualified, our arms wrapped tight around each other.

LEVI: I'll be honest: I was pretty bummed. I'd trained a full year to do this race with my dad. Now this newspaper story was coming out, and I'm not doing the race.

Somehow, I was able to get past that, and realize, "This is my dad's year. *His* story, of overcoming." That's what led to me giving that picture to the newspaper.

TERRY: I'd forgotten all about it. Hadn't even thought about the story coming out. Two days later, we're in Seattle, getting ready for our speaking engagement. I get a text message from a friend—it's the Coeur d'Alene newspaper, the front page! He texted me the article, and I see it for the first time.

I see the photo—*our* photo—of me hugging Levi after being disqualified. "*Terry Gurno Looks to Compete in Ironman After Last*

Year's Effort Fell Short," the first line reads. *Great, more pressure,* I think. Then I see the main headline.

I stare, my eyes wide.

Unfinished Business, the headline says.

LEVI: The newspaper story gave me a new clarity. It helped me swallow the hard pill that I'm not going to be doing the Ironman race with my dad. Now, I became confident he was going to finish. I was able to enjoy the fact that I could just be there and encourage my dad.

TERRY: Now Coach Corey's final training plan was coming into play. Not just my last-minute physical training—my mental training, too. Every day, Corey had me write out what I'm going to do. How long I'm going to be on my feet. What time I'm going to bed. What my morning looks like. What I'm having for breakfast. What time I'm leaving for the course, on race day. What I'm going to do once I hit the course.

Corey had me visualizing the whole race. Putting on my wetsuit. Drinking a Gatorade before I practice my swim. Then the swim. The transition, coming out of the water. Then the bike. Then the run. All the way to that exhilarating moment of crossing the finish line, and throwing my arms up in triumph.

I wrote it all down. And I read it, every day.

The idea was to not think about anything. Don't *think,* Terry. Just *do.*

That was one of the advantages of having a coach. After training so relentlessly, the final push to race day was my mental preparation.

LEVI: I'm certain my dad's bike crash fueled his determination to forget all the noise surrounding him, and focus on the race.

TERRY: The crash didn't put any worries in me about the things I couldn't control. Mechanical failures. Equipment mishaps. What it did do was make me nervous about going downhill.

I found myself braking a lot. Going downhill slow. I knew that wasn't going to work, on race day. As the race approached, I had to work through these issues, or they'd place in my head the possibility of defeat.

The greatest challenge I faced, other than endurance, was my mental state. Letting go of the pressure I'd placed on myself to finish.

Once Levi decided not to do the race he focused all his attention and energy on my race. We were together the whole week. He helped me stay focused, talking me through race week, going down to Ironman Village with me. He was with me when I signed in and got my bib number and race info.

On Saturday he went with me to check my bike in. He carried my transition bags for me, the same way I did for him for his first Ironman.

He was there every step along the way.

LEVI: We had tons of family come into town. My wife's family. My aunt and uncle. There was a lot of anticipation and excitement and pressure on my dad, approaching that day.

TERRY: Around this time, I received a text message from the Ironman organization. Apparently, they'd read the *Unfinished Business* news story. Dave Downey, the race director, found it interesting and thought I might make a good speaker at the opening ceremony.

"You're going to have about five minutes to speak," Dave told me, when we met. "And Terry, I don't want to put any pressure on you, but let me tell you some of the speakers we've had in the past."

He starts rattling off names. Telling me about three-time World Champions, triathlon record holders. "I don't want to put any pressure on you, Terry, but we really need you to deliver something that will light a fire in our competitors."

"Okay, Dave," I shrugged. "I'll do my best."

The opening ceremony comes. Hundreds of people. Ironman competitors, past and present. Video presentations. Finally, Dave runs on stage. Taking the microphone, he tells everybody, "I was reading the newspaper the other day. This front-page story grabbed me. I read it, and thought, *This is what Ironman is really all about! We need to have this guy speaking, at the opening ceremony!*"

Who is this guy Dave's talking about? I'm certain people are wondering to themselves.

"He's here tonight!" Dave says, and he holds up the newspaper. "Here he is, *Mr. Unfinished Business!*"

People are clapping. Cheering. The loudspeakers start booming that song by Bachman-Turner Overdrive, "Taking Care of Business," as I step onto the stage.

I seize the moment to share my story. "I'm here like a lot of you," I say, scanning the crowd of athletes. "My goal is to finish, not to try. I want to be an Ironman. And I'm not going to give up until that happens!"

My whole speech lasted 11 minutes. Longer than Dave had asked. In retrospect, it was 11 minutes that soon defined my life.

People started calling me "Unfinished Business." They came up after the ceremony, clapping me on the back, high-fiving me.

"Unfinished Business!" they shouted.

"Unfinished Business," they smiled, shaking my hand, "that was so good!"

"We know you're going to do it this year!"

"We believe in you!" They put their arms around my shoulders. "You got it, Unfinished Business, you got this!"

The next day, I planned to do a quick workout. A 15-minute swim, 10-minute ride, 10-minute jog. As I'm heading in, people are still coming up to me. "Hey, are you Unfinished Business?"

I guess I am, I thought, smiling matter-of-factly.

I went to the bike corral, to put my bike away for the race. Everybody there recognized me. "Unfinished Business!" They approached, for a fist-bump, an odd smile spread across their face. "We know you got this, big guy. It's all yours, this year. You're going to finish it!"

Their enthusiasm made me feel alive. At the same time, I could feel the pressure building.

Finally, my brother-in-law Dennis came up to me. "Dude," he said, "do you have any idea how much pressure there is on you to finish this?"

I laughed. "I am *very* aware," I said. I truly felt it. *There's no choice now,* I realized. *There's no going back.*

PART FOUR

HOW BAD DO YOU WANT IT?

CHAPTER TWENTY

Race Day

TERRY: The forecast on race day was for wind and heat. Temperatures in the 90s. We'd heard there was a high wind alert, but you never know what that means. It was windy at our house, and it's always even windier at the lake.

2:30 in the morning I woke. Got up. Levi arrived with a friend and made me breakfast. We started going through my pre-race routine.

LEVI: I wasn't living at home. I had a friend, Chase, who wanted to go to the Ironman, so we woke at 2:30 and rode the moped down to my parents' house. I saw my dad going through the same routine we'd had the year before—except this was his race, not mine.

"Hey Dad," I said, "let's go through your special needs bag. Let's make sure you have everything. What's your plan for transition? How often are you going to eat?" Asking him questions, helping him get locked in mentally. Just making sure he was dialed in and good to go, that he was set up for success.

TERRY: It was 4:00 in the morning when I texted Coach Corey. *Have you seen the wind?*

Corey texted me back: *Why are you worried about the wind?*

I laughed. Immediately, he could see I was focused on the wrong thing.

I start visualizing my race. Watching the clock. Three hours before race time. Two and a half hours. Two hours.

I started thinking to myself, *Gurno, you're too excited. You need to lower yourself.* Calming myself down was becoming a challenge, right off the bat.

LEVI: We rode the moped down to Ironman. My dad drove the truck, with my sister. Since I wasn't in this year's race, I wasn't able to go into the athlete's area with him. So that was where we split up.

It was inspiring to watch Dad prepare. The athlete he'd become was a far cry from the athlete he was, a year ago. At one point, he called me over.

"Hey, Bud. I want you to do the body marking on me."

For a moment, I felt this overpowering sense of oneness with my dad. I grabbed the official body marker, and asked if I could mark my dad up. I wrote his number on his arm.

TERRY: Taking a Magic Marker, Levi wrote my number "1662" on both arms. On my left calf, he wrote the number "56." That's the age I was going to be, at the end of the year. It looked like he was having an out-of-body experience, as he did it.

Next, I turned in my two special needs bags.

My bike special needs bag had extra sandwiches. Ice. A frozen Snickers.

In my running special needs bag were socks, candy bars, a long-sleeved shirt, and a sandwich.

I turned in my bags. Went and pumped up the tires on my bike.

Stowed my water bottles on my bike. All my beverages were frozen, because I knew they were going to melt.

I checked my transition bags one last time. My T-1 bag had my bike helmet, my gloves, my sunglasses, my shoes. If they weren't in the bag, too bad for me. It was too late now. I chugged down my Gatorade. Started putting on my wetsuit. When I came out, I saw Levi and together we went down to the water.

We snapped a picture together, before I went in the lake. Once the race started, I wouldn't see Levi again until I was on the bike.

That's when I started thinking about last year's Ironman. Last year was: *I hope I can. I hope I can.* This year, I was more focused. I had confidence in my training. Confidence in my nutrition. From Coach Corey's regimen, I knew I was on pace to make it.

It was a beautiful day. I felt energized by the clean air, the Idaho sun. For a moment, the only sound I was aware of was the bobbing of buoys out on the water and my pounding heart.

Then Levi hugged me. He told me he loved me. "I love you too, Bud," I said.

Levi said, "Today, you're going to be an Ironman! I am going to be here for you every step of the way. Today is your day, you trained for it, run your race!"

"This is it!" I answered with a fist-bump. "I love you, Bud, thank you for everything!"

I went down, and did my practice swim, along with a bunch of other athletes. Hundreds of people were already in the water. The whole beach buzzed with anticipation. In only a few minutes, the National Anthem would play, and the starting gun would go off.

LEVI: He got in position for the swim. He looked focused. Excited. I started praying. I was nervous, but locked in and excited too. I felt more nerves and excitement than if I was the one racing!

TERRY: I was jammed in the crowd of the two-hour swim group. Toward the back of all the swimmers. Feeling fired up. I knew, once the starting gun went off, that it would be nearly 40 minutes before I entered the water.

Squinting across the beach, I scanned for my family. No sight of them.

Around me the other competitors were splashing around. Nervous. Silent. Waiting. Most of them younger. A few my age. Watching each one of them prepare themselves inspired me. I was looking at my fellow competitors and thinking, *Oh man, this is it. This is your day. You got this, buddy.* I'd look somebody in the eye. "Hey man, good luck!" "Hey, is this your first one?" "How are you feeling?" Knowing that if I'm in the back of the pack and they are too, they're not fast swimmers. Swimming is going to be a challenge. But they're ready to do this. To get the job done. To embark on a crazy, holy mission.

Just like me.

LEVI: The swimmers were told to line up. Our family stood above the beach, scanning the water for Dad. There was this quiet energy. I noticed other families locked in embraces, tears streaming down their faces, unable to stand the tension.

For a fleeting moment, I let my mind go back to my goal of finishing Ironman with my dad, completing the dream together. What followed was a rush of guilt, a rush of love for my dad. This was his day. At the end of the day, *he* was going to be an Ironman.

That's when the starting gun cracked. The competitors moved forward.

The race was on.

CHAPTER TWENTY-ONE

The Swim

TERRY: For 40 minutes I stood there. Waiting. Slowly inching forward, like a herd of wetsuited cattle, moving through the starting arch.

The lake was a jumble of swimmers. Splashing. Paddling. Battering the waves. Launching themselves into the churning water, trying to find a lane.

I oriented myself. A lot of swimmers immediately launch themselves into the middle of the lane. My strategy was to swim as close to the buoys as possible, where fewer swimmers were. I'd stay away from the aggressive swimmers, taking my time and easing into my strokes. Trying to relax myself as I move through the water. At the same time, I'm filled with butterflies, my heart is pounding, and my mind throbs with the slap of water.

Calm yourself, Gurno. The butterflies, the nerves, the excitement are so high! My first goal is to relax. Get in rhythm with my swimming.

I hit the water. I'm off to a good start. Get a hundred yards out. 200 yards. Then I stop—not to rest, or because I'm out of breath—but to calm myself. Then I dive under and start swimming again.

Five times I perform this same maneuver, in the first length.

Just to stay relaxed. Just to stay calm.

I'm trying to remain careful, to heed Coach Corey's warnings, since there are swimmers coming up right behind me, thrashing and grunting and spraying water at my back. They slam into me. *Move it, Gurno!* But there's nothing I can do. Frustrated, I try not to beat myself up for making the same mistake as last year. Then I reach the end of the length, turn the corner, find my rhythm again, and stay in that rhythm the whole way back.

Thanks to Corey, my spotting has improved. Every three or four strokes, I take a breath, look up, spotting the shore to get my bearings, to make sure I'm going in a straight line. The year before, I never gave a thought to that at all, and zig-zagged all over the lake. Doing that increased my time, making the course a lot longer than it needed to be.

Because my spotting has improved, I calm down more quickly. Still, I had no idea how I was doing, time-wise. I didn't have a feel for that.

I came out of the water, my first lap completed. I ran up the beach, then back to the water, for lap two. I felt good. I felt confident. I took my time, unflustered, getting back in the water.

About ten strokes into my next lap, I heard a splashing sound. A guy came swimming up beside me, churning up the water aggressively. I probably should have pushed him away. Instead, he elbowed me in the side of the head—*Bam!*—and knocked my goggles off.

I shook my head, dizzy. There was no time to waste. I found my goggles, strapped them on again. Now I had water in my goggles, but I wasn't mad. I regained my composure and returned to swimming again, as fast as I could.

Instantly I found a rhythm that was good for me. But now, I'm being pushed and shoved by other triathletes—a lot of them competing for a good time, a personal record, and not just to finish. You can tell they're frustrated—frustrated that you're slow and you're ahead of them. So they pull and push you aside. They ram you aside, and watch as you plunge underwater.

Frantically, I get out of their way, by moving to an inside position. *That wasn't as bad as the first year,* I think. I reclaim my position. Finish the first quarter of the lap. Then the first half. I'm launching myself easily through the water, in a straight line. Closer and closer I get to the shore, to finishing the swim. As my strokes carry me forward, my mind is racing, wondering what my time is.

LEVI: From the shore, we were looking at over 1,300 athletes, all in wetsuits. I couldn't tell which was my dad, once he hit the water.

Luckily, there's this thing called the Ironman Tracker. I saw it update, when dad went through his first loop of the swim. I could tell he was having a great swim.

TERRY: I knew the time I wanted and what time I wanted to be at my first transition. As I came out of the water, I was fired up. I looked up and saw my time.

I'm 10 minutes faster than last year! Awesome!

LEVI: He was right on pace. Our entire family was yelling and screaming and cheering him on. Hugging each other and taking videos.

He was in the zone. My heart soared. *Okay, he's doing well. He's off to a good start.*

TERRY: Coming out of the water, I felt fantastic. I felt brave. I was determined. I saw my family waiting for me on the shore and they were all fired up and rooting me on. They were yelling at me, "Dad! Yes! You made it!" Levi was yelling, "Awesome swim, Dad!! Great job! Keep it up! You're killing it!" I was fired up!

I hurried up the beach. Into this area called the "wetsuit strippers," where they strip off your wetsuit. Aware of my time, I relaxed into the first transition. I wanted to get my wits about me. To calm my breathing down. *Slow down, Gurno, slow down.* I felt that would be the best use of my energy. What I didn't realize was this wasn't the right approach. In fact, it was the worst move I could make.

And I was setting myself up for disaster.

CHAPTER TWENTY-TWO

The Bike

LEVI: As he was transitioning to the bike, our whole family ran over. Yelling and cheering him on. "You can do it, Dad!" "Way to go, Dad!"

Meanwhile, I'm yelling at him. Coaching him.

"Hey, Dad, make sure you have your water bottle! Make sure you have enough nutrition! Make sure everything's good to go!" Keeping him focused as he started his bike ride.

TERRY: Comfortably coming out of transition, I straddled my bike. Checked my time. Exactly the transition time I wanted. *So far, perfect!*

Then came the wind. Whipping through.

As I started pedaling, the wind whooshed past me, slamming me in the face. That's when I noticed the sponsorship banners that line the course. It's windy, and the banners are sticking straight out.

Wind, that's all I need, I thought. It'd be hard to ignore that wind.

The bike course is laid out like an upside-down letter L. You go six miles northeast, turn around and come back through town. At about the 13-mile mark you get on the highway, head south, then you turn around at the tip of the lake and head back north.

The wind was furious. Unrelenting. The intense headwinds gave me the feeling I was going nowhere. It was definitely impacting my time, I noticed. Slowing me down.

As I was finishing my first loop and coming through town, I approached the halfway point and looked at my watch. In shock, I realized I was 18 minutes behind where I needed to be. I hit the pedals harder, all the while fighting the treacherous wind.

Just keep riding, I thought. *Pedal, Gurno. Pedal.*

As I battled the wind, doubt began creeping in. In my panicked mind I could see my family, setting up their signs back in town. *Go, Terry! Go, Dad! Awesome!* I could hear them yelling, "He's going to do it this year!"

I pedaled harder, trying to stave off disaster.

LEVI: As Dad went on his first 56-mile loop, my family and I followed him on his Ironman Tracker. We could see where he was on the course. Things looked good.

We decided to go into the Coeur d'Alene Resort, and get a little rest. Everybody was exhausted from rising so early. So on his first loop around the lake, we were resting, charging our phones, and keeping a close eye on his tracker.

About three-and-a-half hours later, I knew he'd be coming into town. "Hey, let's all go outside, and cheer Dad on when he's coming through!"

We returned to the course. By now, the wind had picked up. It gusted with power. *No problem.* We're waiting.

And waiting.

"Allright, he's going to be coming any minute," I told everybody, looking at my clock. *He has to be on pace. Dad needs to be coming through any minute.*

We waited. And waited.

Thirty minutes later, Dad comes biking through town.

My whole family spots him. "Yes! Yay! There he is! You're doing great, Dad!"

I felt a sudden, excruciating bolt of panic. I thought, *No, this isn't good. He's 30 minutes behind where he needs to be. He needs to keep moving!*

At this point, something changed in my mentality. I had the realization that Dad could be facing another DNF. He might miss the cut-off again.

Putting my family in my rear-view, I got on my moped. Off I raced, to chase down my dad. I knew I had to tell him he was behind.

I met him at mile 60, the special needs bag station. He saw me coming. I started yelling at him, at the top of my lungs. "Dad! You're 30 minutes behind where you need to be to make the cut-off! You can't stop here!" Because I realized his plan was to stop for five to seven minutes, to stretch, and refuel. "You have to keep going!" I yelled. "Before it's too late!"

TERRY: Because Levi had trained with me, he was aware how I rode. So even before I came biking through town, Levi's worried. He's looking at the clock every few minutes. "Guys, this is not good. This is *not* good. Dad's behind schedule, and he's not going to make it."

All of a sudden, I'm approaching the special needs station. Levi comes screaming up to me on his moped.

"Dad!" he yells. "You've really got to push it, Dad! You don't have any time to spare! You're falling behind the cut-off!"

"I know," I shout back, "but it's this wind! It's brutal!"

"It doesn't matter," Levi insists. "You've got to make up some ground! You can't ease up!"

Levi's right, I think. *But I need my nutrition.* Because of the wind, I was already fading. I needed the special needs station that was coming up to restock my fluids and my nutrition.

Levi must have been reading my mind. "Dad," he yelled at me, "when you get your special needs bag, you can't get off your bike!" Usually, most competitors get off their bike, they'll stretch, eat, take a break. "You've got to eat on your bike," Levi warned me. "And you've got one minute! That's it!"

I nod. Slow down as I'm approaching the special needs station. I get there, and the volunteers hand me my special needs bag. Behind me I see Levi's stopped the moped, about 75 yards away. Just eye-balling me. I didn't know it, but he's timing me. As he sees me starting to get off my bike he yells, "Dad, stay on your bike!"

"Okay!" I holler back. *Great. No time for rest.* So I stay on my bike. The volunteers are holding my special needs bag, desperately handing me whatever I need.

"Okay, Dad!" I hear Levi holler. "Time's up! You gotta go!"

I grimace. Hand the volunteers back the stuff I didn't have time to eat. Pedal off. Away I go on my bike again.

Levi's chasing me down on the moped. Telling me, "Dad, you're behind. You have to stay low!" I'm going uphill—remember, hills are the toughest thing for me—and combined with the wind, it's making my muscles burn with each stroke.

Finally, I start cramping. Cramping bad. Beads of sweat flying off my handlebars. The furious *up, down, up, down* of my pedaling slows. My pace slows. Levi sees this.

"What's the matter?"

"I'm cramping!"

"Dad," Levi groans, "you don't have time to cramp! And you can't slow down! That's not a suggestion!"

"Okay!" I moan, picking up the pace again. "I got it!"

LEVI: "I know you're hurting, Dad!" I said. "I know it's tough, but you have to go faster!"

At that point, I made the decision to be out on the highway the rest of the bike portion, going ahead of him so I could encourage him and coach him up because he was cutting it so close to being disqualified again.

TERRY: At the time, I didn't know it. But right then, Levi's instant messaging on Facebook. "Guys, here's my dad right here," he's posting, on Facebook Live. Streaming it to our family and friends. "He's doing the Ironman, he's going up this hill, and you've got to pray for him!"

I knew I was close to another DNF. I had no idea I was *that* close. So I put my head down, and pedaled desperately. It took all of my concentration to keep pushing through the wind.

Fearful that I wouldn't make it, Levi began texting my wife Nancy. *Dad may not make it, Mom. You need to prepare.*

LEVI: We're headed back to town. Dad's fatigue is increasing. I'm yelling at him and coaching him up, from my moped. I know how Dad rides, and I can tell he's fading. Getting groggy. So every now and then, I just yell, "Dad, get your head up! Don't pay any attention to the wind!"

But the wind's battering him. And now we're at mile 80. Only 10 more miles to the 90-mile cut-off.

The same 90-mile cut-off he was disqualified at, the year before.

CHAPTER TWENTY-THREE

"The Ride of Your Life"

TERRY: Nobody had talked to me about, *What if. What if* I don't make the cut-off. But here I was, cutting it close and facing another DNF.

LEVI: From mile 56 on, I was on the moped. Around mile 75, I'll be honest, I became disheartened. I lost it. Lost my confidence. Lost my conviction we'd reach our goal.

I remember being on the moped, in tears, just praying. "Lord, this can't happen again! This is not what we planned for!" It was the reality of everything—the wind, this massive headwind Dad was fighting.

It's not fair!

That's when I felt a surge of adrenaline. A boost of faith. I stopped thinking, *Maybe he won't finish.* Erasing that mindset, I texted my family.

Everyone needs to be praying. Because it was looking like he might not make the 90-mile cut-off.

Prepare yourselves, is what I was saying. *Pray for strength for Dad.*

I still believed in him. And so I'm out there with him, texting my family *Pray, everybody, pray* and yelling at him. "Don't slow down, Dad! Keep pushing!"

He was two miles now from the 90-mile cut-off. My mind was in and out of fear. I stared at the sky. "Lord, I pray he can do this! Give him strength!"

TERRY: I'm thinking to myself, *I need a break. I need a couple of minutes to just keep pedaling, but not push it. I need rest.*

That's what I'm thinking as I turn the corner, and Levi's parked right there. He's parked on the side of the road, and he waves at me and yells. "Dad, you have to have the ride of your life if you're going to make it back!" He's waving his arms and pointing up the road, urging me to go faster. "There's no time to rest or take it easy!"

Levi doesn't know what I'm thinking. But he knows how I ride. He knows my body is exhausted. I'm fried. He can see the pain on my face. He'd even calculated it out. "You have to average 17.3 miles-an-hour on the way home." I knew that was fast. The good news is, I was battling a headwind coming out, but now there's a tailwind. Now, the wind is *pushing* me. It's propelling me forward.

"Do you feel that tailwind, Dad?"

I nodded. I put my head down, and pedaled as fast as I could. I started picking up speed. Levi's friend Chase was also out there on a moped, and I passed him, so I knew I was going fast.

LEVI: I had ridden to the mile 90 point. I'm waiting there, for my dad. He had a minute and a half to get there, before he missed the cut-off. Before he was disqualified.

I saw him approaching, but he was still a little ways out.

He's cutting it so close! "Dad!" I yelled. "You have one minute to get to that spot!" I pointed to the 90-mile cut-off. "You have to *go!*"

Dad nodded. And he just pushed it. He pushed on. Relying on self-will.

A minute later, he glides by the 90-mile cut-off point.

He made it, with 30 seconds to spare.

TERRY: I finally made it. Levi kept pushing me. He wouldn't let me surrender.

LEVI: I was ecstatic that he made the mile 90 cut-off! I texted my family. *He made it. He made it!*

As he zoomed past me I shouted: "Dad, you made it!" He smiled, and put his head up—not letting up but just catching his breath, because that last mile took so much out of him.

I averaged out the time. Calculated everything. He'd made the 90-mile cut-off, but now he was in danger of missing the next cut-off.

Heading back to town I passed my dad, and yelled at him, "Dad, you made that mile 90 cut-off, but you have to have the ride of your life to make the next cut-off! You have to have the ride of your life to stay in the race!"

TERRY: It took all my effort to keep pushing through the wind. I put my head down, tried not to focus on the searing pain in my legs, yearning for a rest. *Keep going. Keep going.*

LEVI: I knew my dad's tendencies. I could see he was tired. He wanted to let up. And so I was yelling at him, "Dad, put your head down! Dad, stay in your arrow position! Dad, keep going! You can't stop!"

Was this having an impact on him? I hoped so. "You have to go, Dad. You have to go!"

TERRY: Finally, I came to the last hill. Levi said, "Dad, you have to PR it. You have to get a personal record up this hill!"

Now, I'd been up this hill many times, at the 98-mile mark. I'd trained on this hill and this hill is brutal, but Levi says, "You have to go up this hill faster than you've ever done!"

LEVI: And he's doing it. He's averaging 17.2, 17.3 miles-an-hour. We're still 14 miles outside of town and it's the last big hill. An epic ascent. Anyone who's done an Ironman knows this hill is the hardest, most merciless on the course.

I didn't want this hill to beat my dad. I shouted, "Dad, you have to beat this hill! You have to make it to the top of this hill in 16 minutes!"

"Bud, I don't know if I can!" he said.

"Dad, you *can*," I answered. There was nothing left to say. He looked straight at me. Looked me right in the eye and said, "Okay, but I'm going to need you here the entire way."

I said, "Dad, I got you."

He focused up. Started pedaling with all his might up this hill. "Dad, you're doing great! You need to get to that tree in one minute! Let's go, Dad, let's go!"

Every minute, I gave him an update, on the amount of time he had. "You can't sit up. You gotta keep going, Dad. You have to pedal." He'd give me a thumbs-up.

"Dad, you're almost to the top! We're gonna make it! *You're* gonna make it! Get to the top of this hill in the next two minutes, and you'll make it to town, I promise you!"

I knew he would. He kept pushing. And pushing.

When we were on that last hill, a cop passed me. He flagged me down. "Hey, you! You shouldn't be out here! It's dangerous!"

I threw up my hands and yelled back, "Hey, officer, I'm sorry, but this moped has a really bad horsepower problem!" Pretending like I was barely able to get it up the hill. The cop narrowed his eyes at me, smiled, then zoomed off.

My dad turned to me, like he couldn't believe his ears. "Did you just get yelled at?"

"Dad, don't worry about it," I said. "Keep going!" I gunned the moped, and we kept climbing. Up, up, up.

Inch by inch toward the top of the hill.

TERRY: All the way up, my body is talking to me, saying *Pain, pain, pain.* I'm thinking to myself, *This is what you have to do, Gurno, if you're going to conquer this hill.*

So I did. By the time I reached the top, I heard Levi shout:

"Dad, you *did* it! That was a personal record!"

My legs screamed for rest, but I felt great. I came up on these other three riders, who were struggling. I pedaled faster, to catch them. Just as I'm approaching, I hear Levi shout, "Hey you guys! You're on the verge of being cut-off! If you don't hurry up, you're going to be disqualified!"

He's talking to the three guys and encouraging them, the same way he's been talking to me. "You guys have to decide right now if you want this or not! You have to pick up the pace!"

All three guys started kicking it up a notch. Grinding their gears to make the cut-off.

LEVI: Dad makes it to the top of the last hill. I'm texting my family. *He's going to make it.* At the same time, I'm telling him, "Dad, you have 10 miles to go. You're going to make it but you can't let up." He's within minutes of not making the final cut-off.

TERRY: Six miles to go. Then five. Then four. Three. Two.

I get back to Northwest Boulevard. Now I'm on the home stretch. A mile away. I turn back to the park and I see stretching ahead of me the bike finish line.

LEVI: We turned onto Northwest, a mile away, and that's when I knew. *Okay, he's going to make it.* I was one street up, on the moped, on a higher street so I could look down on the street he was on, and watch him finish. I started yelling at the top of my lungs. "Dad, you're going to do it. You're going to do it. *You did it!*" I was so emotional and filled with joy. I was so proud!

TERRY: I made the bike cut-off by just under three minutes. So did the other guys Levi was talking to. They would have missed the cut-off, if it wasn't for Levi.

LEVI: At this point, I'd been following him for 56 miles. Not letting up. Yelling, coaching, training, encouraging. I was emotional, nervous, excited, fearful, hopeful . . .

It was 56 miles of not knowing whether he'd make it. A gigantic test of faith. When I realized he'd made the cut-off by just a couple of minutes, I shouted. "Thank you, Lord, he did it!"

TERRY: Now I'm just beside myself, feeling reawakened, because I'd never made it this far.

I climb off the bike. Hurry to the second transition. Get my bag, and I go in the tent, and there's a volunteer helping me get all my gear for the run.

My knees are burning. I'm in extreme pain. On my first loop on the bike, I'd fallen. I was going up the hill, and got tangled into some other riders. I fell and slammed my left knee. The weight of my entire body was absorbed by it. The knee throbbed, and the muscles stabbed me with each stroke, but because I was riding my bike and focused on finishing it didn't hurt, at the time.

LEVI: I swung off the moped. Ran to meet my family at the transition area. When I got there, I broke down in tears—tears of exhaustion, and for all I'd just experienced. Tears of not knowing if my dad was going to make it or not.

TERRY: I figured: *I'm going to find out how much my knee hurts, when I start running.* So I get my transition bag. Lace up my running shoes. I'm ready to go.

During the transition period, there's this guy sitting behind me and he's not doing well. He barely made the bike cut-off. He's in immense pain, dehydrated, and exhausted. One of the volunteers asked if anybody had salt.

"I have salt," I said.

"I don't have any salt," the guy said. I gave him my salt. He took a couple of fingertips full, and instantly looked better. I asked if he was good to go.

"I'm good," he said.

I got my salt and went out. Levi and my whole family were waiting for me. Rooting me on.

That's when I found out how much time I had left.

I had been training for a seven-hour marathon. It's more of a walk than a run. That seemed realistic for me, so I figured I needed seven hours.

Well, I didn't have seven hours. I only had six and a half.

Six and a half hours, or I'd fail my second Ironman.

LEVI: Dad came hustling out of the transition. He looked exhausted, but upbeat.

"Dad, how do you feel?"

"Man, I'm tired," he groaned.

I hugged him and said, "Dude, you did it! You just had the bike ride of your life!"

That's when I knew I had to break the news to him. I knew he'd trained for a seven-hour marathon. Even at seven hours, it wasn't going to give him any margin for error. He was already behind. I couldn't run the race for him, but I could do my part. As he readied to go out on the run, our eyes locked.

"Dad, good job. You just had the ride of your life. Now you need to have the run of your life." I pulled out my watch. "You have six and a half hours to finish this race."

CHAPTER TWENTY-FOUR

The Run

TERRY: My legs were throbbing. My knees felt ripped up. I knew I'd hurt myself bad, on the bike. *At least you made the cut-off,* I thought to myself.

I took my first step to start the marathon. *Man, that really hurts!* Levi came running up.

"Dad, don't run," he said. "Take a couple of hundred yards' walk, get your legs underneath you."

I said, "My knee really hurts. I don't know if I can run."

"Well, just walk right now," Levi said.

We started walking. Levi went with me for a hundred yards. Then another hundred. "You got this," he said, pleased with my stride. "Okay, Dad, I'll be rooting for you," and he left, to rejoin the family.

Off I limped. I tried running a couple of times, but I just couldn't. My knee was in so much pain. Instead, I walked as fast as I could.

Mile one. Then mile two.

At mile 2.5, Coach Corey saw me. He'd been tracking me, on the race. He flagged me down.

"How are you doing?"

I didn't lie. "I'm not doing good," I groaned. "My knee is killing me."

I headed up the course. Mile three. Mile four. Further out, I saw another couple of friends. They asked how I was doing, and I complained about my knees.

For my run, I'd packed twelve Ibuprofen pills for the day. The goal was to use twelve, for the entire day.

I started taking those. Gulping them down.

LEVI: I ran with him for the first three-quarters of a mile. Knowing the Ironman run is broken into three 8.7-mile chunks, and that he seemed to be doing well, I said, "Allright, Dad. I'm going to go inside and eat." I hadn't eaten all day. I was dehydrated. "I'm going to be here waiting for you, after your first eight-mile loop. Here's the pace that you need to keep."

I joined my family. We ate, and talked about Dad's race, about the bike ride. "Man, that was crazy!" Talking about how Dad needed to have an amazing run. Meanwhile, my mind's flashing to my dad, out on the course. Quickly I finished eating, and hurried out. Something's telling me, *I need to be there, I need to be with Dad.*

TERRY: I'm gulping down Ibuprofen. Not taking them all at once, but pretty consistently. Still, the pain ramps up. Every step sends pain shooting down my legs.

Six miles into the run, Coach Corey comes up to me again.

"Terry, do you want to know what the time cut-offs are?"

"No," I said. I thought, *What does it matter? I'm going to do the best I can.* So I told Corey, "No, I don't want to know."

Corey gives me a stern eye. "I want you to know," he says, in a serious voice.

I didn't have enough energy to argue. "Okay," I said.

"Your first cut-off is 9:00 tonight," Corey said. "By that time, you need to finish your second loop of the marathon. That's about 18 miles in." He shot me another humorless look. "But Terry, you've got your work cut out for you, because right now, you may not make it."

Again I said, "Okay." And I started walking, as fast as I could.

LEVI: I'm keeping up with Dad, on his Ironman Tracker. I know where he is. I notice he's coming back towards town, to finish his first loop.

And again, he's cutting it close.

Truth is, he's actually *slower* than he needs to be. He's not on pace to finish in time.

He's running on fumes, I think. I wait for him, around the corner, as he's approaching mile 8.

"Dad, you're doing great," I shout out. "How are you feeling?"

"Levi," Dad gasps, "I'm in a lot of pain." Because he had fallen on his bike. "My knee is hurting."

TERRY: By the time I had finished my first loop, I'd taken all my Ibuprofen. At mile 8, Levi came jogging up to me.

"Dad," he said, "you're doing good. You're doing good, Dad. But here's the deal. You just had the bike ride of your life, but you need to have the run of your life, too. You've got to pick up the pace, so you can make it."

Pick up the pace?

"You can do it, Dad," Levi insisted, sounding like a five-star general. "You just *gotta* do it."

Now all my other kids—Chelsea, Ali, Christian and Sarah—had

ridden bikes and mopeds out to find me at different points in the run. All during the run, I could hear them yelling, encouraging me. "We believe in you, Dad! We believe in you!" as I passed them. Then they would go up another mile and do it again. It fired me up big time.

Meanwhile Levi continued next to me, coaching me up.

He'd look at me and say, "Dad, you have to run! You need to start running right now."

So I did. I started running. Levi talking to me the whole time. "It's all mindset, Dad. It's all in your mind, and you've got to break through every barrier right now, to go the distance." Trying to encourage me.

He did.

He encouraged me for the next 14 miles. Nine of them in flip-flops. He didn't leave my side.

LEVI: I noticed he was walking. I said, "Dad, you can't walk. You have to jog."

"Levi, I can't," he grimaced, rubbing his knees. "I'm in a lot of pain."

"Dad, I understand that. But your leg is going to hurt," I said, "regardless if you finish or not. So the question is, do you want it to hurt as a finisher? Or someone who didn't make it?"

He stared at me. I could see Dad switch off that voice in his head that was urging him to quit. "I want to finish," he said.

"Then you have to run," I told him. "You have to keep running." I told him how proud I was, trying to distract him from the pain. "I know it hurts. But pretty soon, your legs are going to go numb. I promise, you won't feel it, but if you want to finish this race, you have to run."

So he started running.

CHAPTER TWENTY-FIVE

No Time To Take It Easy

TERRY: Another friend, Dave Miller, one of my closest friends in the world, joined Levi then.

LEVI: Dave and I start running alongside my dad. My plan wasn't to keep running with him. It was to run with him to McEuen Park, a half-mile loop where everyone can wait. But I realized how close he was to being disqualified.

So I ended up running 14 miles with him. Running in flip-flops, because I had nothing on my mind other than my dad finishing.

TERRY: Dave Miller ends up running 18 miles with me. All the time, he's encouraging me.

"You're doing really good," Dave says, smiling, "really, really good!"

Levi knows I'm not doing good. But Miller is trying to be encouraging. I hear them bantering among themselves, talking behind me so I can't hear.

"Miller," Levi says, "don't tell him he's doing good. He's *not* doing good! Tell him he's going too slow. He needs to pick it up."

Now Dave is one of the nicest guys in the world. He doesn't want to hurt my feelings. So now, Levi is talking to me, every half mile, because I'm taking my time.

"Dad," he says impatiently, with his flip-flops *slap-slapping* the pavement. "You're not okay. You gave up a little bit there." He's getting more and more nervous. "Dad, you've got to keep this pace!"

LEVI: Dave and me, we're running with my dad, trying to keep him from shutting down, really coaching him up.

I say, "Hey, Dad, you've gotta run to that sign. You can do a run/walk combo, but you have to run to that sign before you can stop."

I'm checking my watch. "Hey, Dad, you have to pick up the pace. You have to *run*."

TERRY: The cut-off time is getting tight. Now it's getting to that time in the race where they bring a race official out. He's the guy who disqualifies you. He's the guy who says to you, "You're out."

And now that guy is out on the track. He's eyeballing me.

And I'm closer and closer to the cut-off and my friends and family are there, they're all yelling and screaming for me. "Go, Dad!" "Go, Terry!"

LEVI: We're running together. Suddenly we're approaching McEuen Park, where there's a cut-off.

"Dad," I say, "you have a minute and a half to get to that cut-off!" We're a little ways away, and I say, "You can't walk. You absolutely *cannot* walk. We have to get to that cut-off or they're going to disqualify you, you're not going to finish."

Dad grinds his teeth. Gets a boost. Hobbles past the race official. He makes it. By—I'm not kidding—30 seconds.

TERRY: You would've thought I was winning the whole race! The way everybody was yelling and cheering and screaming. "Here he comes, oh my gosh, he's getting closer, he's going to make it! *He's going to make it!*"

They're all yelling and cheering, and it's just so I can make my last lap! My brother-in-law is standing next to Nancy, and he's got tears in his eyes. He looks at Nancy, and says, "He still has one more lap to go!" as I head to my special needs bag, needing more than anything to grab a break, a rest, a moment to ease my pain.

I didn't get a chance.

LEVI: Dad makes this cut-off, and we're running and running. At this point, I know what my dad needs. Dave Miller, who's still running with us, is being too encouraging.

"Terry," he'd tell my dad, "you're doing great. You're doing so good!" But I'm the one saying, "No, Dad. You're *not* doing good. You need to go faster! *Faster!*" because I know my dad.

I wasn't breaking him down. I was building him up. I wasn't being mean, I was challenging him to succeed, because that's what he needed in that moment.

"Dad, if you don't pick up the pace, you're not going to finish this race. Do you want to come this far just not to finish?"

"No," he said.

"Then you have to pick up the pace," I said. "You have to keep going."

TERRY: The volunteers tossed me my special needs bag. "Here. Take whatever you need. You can't stop." I had to get my nutrition and my drink out while I walked—and I had only 75 yards where I could walk.

Now, my run and my walk weren't that much different, at this point. But I kept going. Levi and Miller are still with me. I tell Levi

I'm hurting again. By this time, my whole body is cramping and on fire with shooting and stabbing pains.

Levi shook his head and said to me, "Dad, here's the deal. You're going to hurt no matter what. Tomorrow, you're gonna hurt. The thing you have to ask yourself, Dad, is this: do you want to hurt as an Ironman, or do you want to hurt as disqualified? Because you have to make that decision, right now."

I said, "I want to hurt as an Ironman."

"Then you've got to go. And keep going."

My whole marathon has been run/walk/pain. Run/walk/pain. I chug down my Gatorade. Pray it will bring me back to life. My body is overheated. My ribs ache. The pain in my knees is excruciating now.

Miller knows without a word being spoken the pain I feel. He smiles and says to me, "How does it feel to accomplish the greatest physical feat of your life at this age?"

I groan and answer, "It's awesome."

Dave says, "Well, it's not gonna happen if you don't hurry up!" Just doing everything he can to push me to give it all I had.

I gave it.

CHAPTER TWENTY-SIX

The Final Lap

TERRY: Right onto 8th Street. Left on Pine. Right on 10th Street. Left on Mountain. Back onto 10th Street. Left on East Lakeshore Drive.

The miles limp by.

Mile after mile, the pain increases. Fewer and fewer competitors are left. The others have finished their race, and gone home. The sky is black, the race course dark, the heat still oppressive.

Levi and Dave are still with me. But I'm talking to myself. *Don't quit. Don't worry about being tired. Find a positive attitude. Finish the race. Don't let your family down.*

LEVI: At mile 22, it's the turnaround point to head back into town to the finish line.

The Ironman corporation—because they had seen the newspaper article and they'd asked my dad to speak at the opening ceremonies, where he became known as Mr. Unfinished Business—because they knew our story, they'd asked if I would put the Ironman medal around his neck, at the finish line. If he made it.

TERRY: They wanted to take Levi back to the finish line, because of the story in the paper. The thing I'd talked about in the opening ceremonies was the dream of Levi placing my Ironman medal around neck.

So they brought a car out for Levi. Levi tells Miller, "Dude, you've got to get my dad to the finish line." He added: "It's on *you,* Miller!" So now, he's putting all the weight of me finishing on Miller's shoulders. And Miller's really nice!

Levi leaves. Now it's just Miller and me. We're racing together. Running together. Hobbling together.

Miller says, "I just can't let your family down here. And you're the deciding factor. Whatever you can do to help me out, man, I'd really appreciate it!"

It was a different kind of encouragement. But it worked.

On the way back, I hit mile 24. Miller says to me, "Terry, you can't walk anymore. It's too close. You have to run, the rest of the way."

Two miles remained. I hadn't run one mile, without stopping, let alone two miles. *I can't run that far!*

My legs were numb. 17 hours of swim, pedal, run. I'd overcome so much. Somehow, I had to overcome this.

LEVI: As my dad approached mile 22—which was the last cut-off—he was so close to *not* making the cut-off that they were picking up orange cones behind him as he's running. They were yanking people off the course. Cutting people off the course, disqualifying them, right behind him.

That's how close he was.

They were saying, "Anyone behind this guy is done." They even told my dad, "Hey, if you don't make it to mile 22 by this time, you're done!"

He hustled. Picked up the pace. And made it by seconds.

That's when coach Corey brought out a car, to take me back to town. I looked at my dad.

"Dad," I said, "I know you can do this. I'm going to be at the finish line waiting for you. You're going to be an Ironman, but you have to pick it up. You have to go fast."

I gave Dave my watch, so he could pace my dad. "Dave," I said, "I know you want to be really nice right now. But the nicest thing you can do for him is make sure he doesn't let up, and get him to the finish line."

Dave took it seriously. "Allright, Terry," he said, strapping on the watch. He looked up the long straightaway, then to my dad, who was laboring. "Here we go. You can't let me down."

TERRY: 1.5 miles to go. A mile and a half to the finish line.

I focused on running as far as I could, for as long as I can.

At that point, Levi had called his friend, Luke Szymanski, the guy who inspired Levi to run his first Ironman.

LEVI: "You've gotta help my dad make this," I told Luke.

TERRY: Luke finds me on the course and starts jogging with me. Encouraging me. He says to me, "Terry, there comes a point in every endurance athlete's race where they think they don't have anything left. But they do." He points up the road. "You have to find that something, right now."

I ran, dragging my feet. *I've got to pull this out*, I thought. *Keep the focus. Keep running, and don't stop.*

A mile out, there's one last station. You can get something to drink and a snack. Every station, I'd grabbed a snack of oranges. I'd grab chicken broth with a Red Bull chaser. Every one.

I come to the last one, and it's so close to the 17 hours now. Luke says, "You don't get to have anything here. The next rest stop is the finish line. Nothing until the finish line, that's your next aid station!"

LEVI: It was so close. We didn't know if he was going to finish in 17 hours or not.

TERRY: I felt like I was going to faint, from the exertion. Miller had told me earlier, "Terry, when you come to the finisher's chute, at the finish line, don't race through like a lot of people do, because you've worked hard for this moment. Take your time. Experience it. Take it all in."

Now, with the finish line up ahead, he told me, "You can't do that now. You *can't* take your time. As a matter of fact, you can't touch anybody. No high-fives, no shaking hands, no fist-bumps, no hugs. There isn't time!"

I broke into a run, my legs floundering. "In fact," he continued, "I don't want you to take this the wrong way, but I'm going to tell your family not to meet you anywhere close to the finish line. Family and friends always want to hug you, before the finish line. I'm going to tell them not to."

"Okay," I grunted.

My hips swung forward, each step filling me with intense pain. Somehow, I didn't collapse. Suddenly, I noticed I'm heading back through McEuen Park for the last time. I scan the course for other competitors. Nobody's around. I run up and across the bridge toward Sherman Avenue. Sherman Avenue is the finish line. I'm running alone through the park. It's quiet. Just the sound of my gasping breath, and my thumping heart.

Now I'm five blocks away from the finish line.

Suddenly I pass a friend, Kevin Pickford. He looks at me and sees I'm struggling, my every step stabbing me with anguish, gasping with every breath. So he texts my brother-in-law: *Terry just passed me. And I don't think he's going to make it. He looks really bad.*

I run, not even sure my feet are touching the ground. Out of the darkness, I hear the Ironman announcer. His voice booming up on Sherman, growing louder and louder, making me feel intensely alive. *Almost there.*

I turn the corner. Up ahead, I can see the finishing chute. The finish line. I see a crowd of people. Making noise and waving their arms. Pounding the sides of the barriers and screaming at me.

I push myself, barely able to stay upright. *Suck it up,* I tell myself. *You're almost there!* I run. Getting closer. Trying to stay on my feet but it's impossible. I'm too exhausted. My kidneys ache. I'm bent over to the right side. My last ounce of energy is wavering.

In a panic, I notice the clock is off. *Oh no! Is the race over? Did I come all this way, only to be disqualified again?*

Dizzy with fear, I stagger forward. The finish line seems to grow smaller, then fades away. Two words flash before my eyes. *Defeat. Doom.* My dream is dead. I'm going to have to sign up for another Ironman tomorrow!

LEVI: For the last four miles, I've been waiting at the finish line. Watching the time tick down. Minutes passing. The 17-hour cutoff approaching.

I'm nervous. People are calling my family. Letting them know, "Hey, he's two miles out!" "Hey, your dad's one mile out!"

I'm standing behind the finish line. Over the crowd, I hear the race announcer's worried voice as he's talking to a race official. "Hey, is he going to do it? Is he going to finish? Where is he? Is he coming?"

All the competitors have crossed the finish line. All except my dad.

It's almost midnight. At midnight, the race is over, and he'll be disqualified, all this for nothing, another year he's sacrificed only to have to try it again.

The crowd roars. Half a mile away, I spot a tiny figure, staggering and weaving up Sherman. The roar of the crowd seems to energize him, as he lumbers toward the finish line. "Dad!" I yell. Every ounce of my being yelling, *Hurry! Come on, Dad!* Overhead, the race announcer's voice is booming. "Okay everybody, let's cheer Mr. Unfinished Business on! He's coming around the corner. He can hear us!"

CHAPTER TWENTY-SEVEN

"You Are An Ironman!"

TERRY: I can barely stand upright. My eyes blur. My head is swimming. Doomed thoughts. *Gurno, you're going to have to sign up for next year. You failed your family. Again. And you've come so close!*

Suddenly, I hear the announcer's voice. Booming. Loud. I look up Sherman, but the lights are too bright and they're making my head pound. I stagger closer, to where I can see the finisher's chute, and a crowd of people screaming. I hear the announcer call my name. "Terry Gurno!" I hear, coming out of my fog. "Terry Gurno, from Coeur d'Alene, Idaho . . ."

I run.

LEVI: Now I see my dad. He makes the turn. He's running up Sherman. Running, then walking, then limping. *He's hurt,* I think. He's hobbling like his leg is broken. He's in tremendous pain. He has nothing left to give, nothing left for the finish.

The crowd roars. Cheering him on. I see my dad make a last spurt toward the finish line. I just stand there. Transfixed. Focused. Praying. *Dear Lord, please!* Praying harder. *Lord, please! He can't let up. Not now!*

TERRY: My legs wobble. I begin to falter, my feet tripping on the blacktop. *Feet, don't fail me now!* I need a final push.

Up ahead, I see the finish line. It fades in and out of my focus. Bombarding my ears is the song "We Will Rock You," booming over the loudspeakers as I nearly topple, nearly crumple, then stagger forward, encouraged by the people screaming and cheering me in.

With my last surge of energy, I weave back and forth, walking, jogging, gasping through the finisher's chute.

With a final push, I cross the finish line.

I hear the announcer bellow: "Terry Gurno, from Coeur d'Alene, Idaho . . . *YOU ARE AN IRONMAN!*"

I throw my arms up. In exhausted triumph. Gasping. My body falling forward. Ready to collapse.

And I see Levi there waiting for me.

LEVI: People are going nuts. Our family is screaming. "He finished! Dad finished!" I see Dad's neon-yellow jersey coming toward me, his face dazed in anguish and exhaustion.

With a minute and a half to spare, he finishes the race. With no one there to hold him upright, he races toward me, then collapses into my arms. He falls into my arms, exhausted and exhilarated, and I'm crying. I'm weeping.

TERRY: Levi comes running up to meet me. I have nothing left. I fall into his arms, and he's holding me up. He's crying. "You did it, Dad! *You did it!*" He's sobbing and shaking. I don't have the strength to cry or I would've been crying too.

LEVI: I'm losing it. "You did it, Dad! You did it! I'm so proud of you!" He's wiped out, too drained to even talk. After we hug and embrace for a minute, I grab the medal and I put it around his neck, and I tell him, "You did it, Dad. You're an Ironman!"

TERRY: Levi's crying and he's talking to me and telling me I did it. "I'm so proud of you, Dad!" I don't know how long we held each other like that. Then Levi goes and gets my medal and places it around my neck.

That was the moment we had talked about. Dreamed about. Him being there. Placing that medal around my neck. He hugged me and told me how much he loved me.

That's when I overheard the race officials. One of the officials, one of the people on staff said to the other, "Go to the official time-keeper, and find out if he's a finisher or not."

LEVI: It was the most surreal thing I've ever experienced in my life. The whole time he was running, biking, battling the wind and intense pain, for 140.6 miles. The grit he had was crazy.

He almost missed every cut-off. But he never stopped. And we were there. Our whole family. Helping to pull him out of those hopeless moments, when his mind was telling him to give up. Ultimately though, it was my dad who had to put in the work to train, to run the race, and to harness the inner strength, the will to finish against everything in his path.

When I look at things like that—that he had Dave and Luke and me right next to him, and our whole family praying, cheering him on, encouraging him—it's just such a testimony to his resilience. His resolve to see the dream realized was insane.

TERRY: "Find out if he's a finisher," I overheard.

I knew I was the final athlete. The last competitor on the course. Levi's placed the Ironman medal around my neck. He had this huge Levi smile on his face, this smile that said, *I'm so proud of you, Dad.* He was the one who challenged me. The one who showed me this was possible, and taught me to face my fears. He's the one posting things on Facebook—*My dad did his first sprint triathlon. I'm so proud of him. Today my dad rode one hundred miles and he'd never done that before*—all culminating in a son's smile that told me *I'm so proud of you for doing this and for wanting it, for going after it, for failing and not giving up.* I could see all of that, in Levi's face.

As he put the medal around my neck he said, "Dad, me being there for you, to support you, meant more to me than finishing my own Ironman."

Now I'm being interviewed by the news. They're taking my picture. And I still don't know if I finished in time.

LEVI: The photographer's taking our picture together. I can see my dad's preoccupied. Looking around.

"Dad? Are you okay?"

He gently lays a hand on my shoulder. "Yeah, Bud, I'm okay." Then he goes to our family, and gives everyone a hug and a kiss.

TERRY: I'm being mobbed by people. Friends. My family. I hear Dave Downey, the announcer, talking about my story, what happened the year before, me coming back. Wanting to do it again and how it all played out. I have this nickname, "Unfinished Business," and every time people slap me on the back they'd say, "Hey, Unfinished Business!" That's what they dubbed me because of one interview and now I'm being interviewed again and that's when a guy comes up to me, he taps me on the shoulder, and says, "Have you heard?"

Heard? I'm puzzled. "No," I say, "I haven't heard." I don't know what he's talking about. "Have I heard what?"

"We didn't know if you were official or not," says the guy. "So I went back to check the time. And I just want you to know you're official. You made it. You're an Ironman."

PART FIVE

FINISHED BUSINESS

CHAPTER TWENTY-EIGHT

Conclusions

TERRY: It's more about the journey than the destination.

So many moments go into telling a story like this. I recall standing at the Ironman finish line, drained of everything, spent, slumped over with fatigue. This guy comes running up to me. He reaches for my hand, and says, "Hey, my name's Kevin. I won the race today." He's pumping my hand up and down like I'm a celebrity. "I wanted to meet you," he says, "because you inspire me, and I would love to have my picture taken with you!"

He'd finished the race eight hours before me. Yet my efforts—to drive my body to the limit of my endurance, to complete the race, to be the last-place finisher—inspired *him*.

That meant a lot to me.

There are so many lessons in reaching for a dream.

When I was training for Ironman, and realized I wasn't prepared, that I was embarking on a journey that might be doomed, I was bummed.

Disappointed.

Frustrated.

Yet Coach Corey helped me dig deep down, and recognize it was a test, that I couldn't conquer my fears of finishing if I didn't overcome them at the starting line. *Terry, focus on what you* can *do. Focus on what you can do to get better.*

I think people look down on defeat. On failure. We beat ourselves up for our past losses, where we're at in life, and get overwhelmed when we feel like we are not far enough along on the journey.

That robs us of the ability to see what we're capable of doing in the meantime. What we have to work on.

Focus on what you *can* control. Most of us have greater clarity about what we *can't* do, what we *don't* have, what's *not* possible. We lack the clarity to see what we *can* do.

What's *possible.*

It's the possibility of our dreams that fuels us with the ability to overcome these insurmountable odds, and achieve the impossible.

Levi wanted it for me. He wanted it desperately. So did my family. My kids banded together to support me. They rallied behind me on the run, on bikes, on mopeds. They cheered me throughout the race, rooting for me. "Dad, we believe in you!" "Dad, you can do it!"

My family wanted it badly. Yet no matter how badly somebody wants it for you, nobody can want it *more than you.*

You're the one in it. Living it. Breathing it. The one who has to walk the walk, run the race. The one who has to stay in it.

Nobody can want your dream more than you.

LEVI: For me, it was all about one decision: the desire to grow in every aspect of my life—spiritually, physically, mentally, and emotionally. The journey is where that growth took place. The decision I made, each and every day, to keep moving forward, is where that growth took place.

You have your own decision to make. If you have a desire to grow, to challenge yourself—if you have a dream that needs to be reawakened—you have to make a choice.

It requires action. It will take commitment, determination, drive, grit. You'll experience ups and you'll experience downs. But that's part of the journey. The pursuit of your dream is the journey!

What is it for you? What dream needs to be reawakened? Don't listen to what the world is saying. Don't listen to the voice in your head telling you that you *can't*. You *can!*

I believe in you. But you need to believe in yourself. And you've got to want it bad! During that final Ironman, I wanted it so bad for my dad . . . but no one could want it more than him. In the end, his grit and determination to never give up led him across the finish line.

Go do it! Live your dream and inspire others. And don't forget to enjoy the journey. Smile every mile!

TERRY: In the end, it was really Levi who fueled the dream. Levi, my son, is the heart of this book.

It was Levi's courage to face his own fears and failures that inspired me. It was him committing a year of his life to his first Ironman. Watching his transformation, seeing the growth that took place and the man he became. It was Levi listening to me talk about my old buried dream. He caught my dream and reawakened it. He rescued it. Levi took away my excuses and asked me that simple, unforgiving question: "Yes, or no?"

My son Levi became my coach and mentor. When I failed the first time, he spurred me to press on. When I committed to racing a second Ironman, Levi guided me through the next year. He knew I was behind after the first bike loop, and left the family to follow me, ride alongside me, wait for me and encourage me. Levi had been in the arena, he'd faced it as a young warrior, and knew the battle I was in. He ran 14 miles beside me, encouraging me, helping me push through the pain. He caught me at the finish line, held me up until I could stand on my own, then placed my Ironman medal around my neck. He kept me focused on the finish line, on my dream.

Levi was the difference-maker. He is the heart and soul of this book. He carried the torch, when this old warrior was ready to surrender. In the end, that is our story.

I know competing in an Ironman isn't for everyone—but there's something for everyone. What's your Ironman? What's that dream that's buried inside of you? What fears and doubts are holding you back? What failures do you need to face?

Face them. Identify your excuses, and answer this question: *Do you want it or not?*

If the answer is yes—if it scares you and excites you at the same time—you're in for a great journey. Surround yourself with the right people. Focus on where you want to go and what you can do. And don't give up 'til you finish!

If our book has helped you on your own journey, I hope you will consider giving a copy to five people you know and care about. Give it to a friend, a co-worker, or a family member. Share it with your son, your daughter, your mother, your father. Who do you know that might benefit from this book and its message? This is a great place to start making a difference for them.

<u>FIVE PEOPLE YOU KNOW</u>
<u>AND CARE ABOUT</u>

1.

2.

3.

4

5.

—TERRY & LEVI GURNO, FATHER'S DAY 2018

— ACKNOWLEDGEMENTS —

We want to thank all those who played a role in our journey. Their love, support, encouragement, prayers, positive vibes and good energy helped us to overcome the odds and finish. We love you and are so thankful you are in our life:

Nancy Gurno, Sarah Gurno, Chelsea Gurno, Ali and Christian Klundt

Pam and Dennis Ranch

Luke Syzmanski

Sam Barnes

Chase Estes

Mike Rima

Chris Lauri

Scott and Denise Clare

Mike and Mary Syzmanski

Coach Corey McKenna

Eric Bogdanowicz

Beau and Nick Snider

Cody Spencer

Katherine Morgan

Daniel Condreay

Mark Hayden

Dave Miller

Dave Scammell

Gene Valenzuela

We also thank the many others who watched, cheered, prayed and supported us during this journey. We felt it, and we know we could never have done it without all of you!

Sam Severn

When we decided to write our book, we prayed for the right person. We met Sam via email. It was these words which captured our attention:

"My calling is helping people rescue and reawaken their old lost dreams—the book ideas they felt too overwhelmed to write, or the screenplay that has been sitting unfinished in a bottom drawer somewhere. I love telling human stories of personal triumph over insurmountable obstacles. It's an honor to help people climb their creative mountains and make those abandoned dreams come true."

When we read those words, we knew we had found the person to tell our story. Thank you, Sam, for using your gifts and your art to climb this mountain with us and to see our dream come true!

— CONTACT —

Thank you for reading our book. Our prayer is
that it inspires you to go after your dreams,
or to help someone go after theirs. We have
one life to live. Let's make it count!

Our mission is to help people WIN in work and life.

If you're looking for inspiration to motivate your team,
company or industry to action, we'd love to be a part
of your event. To book us or to learn more about our
keynote talks, contact us through our website.
You can also follow us on social media:

TERRY & LEVI GURNO
www.terrygurno.com
PHONE: 208-277-9706
FOLLOW US AT:

TWITTER: @terrygurno, @levigurno
FACEBOOK: terry.gurno, levi.gurno.1
INSTAGRAM: terry_gurno, levigurno_